HOPE
for ALL

*Ten Reasons
God's Love Prevails*

GERRY BEAUCHEMIN

Hope For All: Ten Reasons God's Love Prevails
Copyright © 2018 Gerry Beauchemin
Malista Press, PO Box 6271, Brownsville, TX 78523
ISBN 978-0-9772793-5-7

All rights reserved.

Unless noted, Bible quotes are from the New King James Version © 1979, 1980, 1982 by Thomas Nelson, Inc. All rights reserved.

Contents

Contents 3
Agony of a Young Girl and a Bible Scholar Icon 5
Acknowledgments 9
Foreword 11
About the Book 12
Abbreviations 13
Preface 15
ANCHOR 1   Hope in History 17
ANCHOR 2   Hope in Fire 27
ANCHOR 3   Hope in Judgment 37
ANCHOR 4   Hope in Ancient Greek 47
ANCHOR 5   Hope in Death 61
ANCHOR 6   Hope in Justice 73
ANCHOR 7   Hope in Our Father 87
ANCHOR 8   Hope in God's Nature 95
ANCHOR 9   Hope in God's Promises 105
ANCHOR 10   Hope in Prophecy 115
Ten Anchors Summarized 127
Bible Interpretation 128
Questions Considered 130
Author Invitation 147
About the Author 148
Notes 151

Agony of a Young Girl and a Bible Scholar Icon

The word "gospel" means "good news," but sadly, for millions of people, it's *not* good news. What's good about being told that you or someone you love might suffer forever after death?

To illustrate the depressing effect the fear of hell brings to people of all ages and backgrounds, reflect a moment on the heartache suffered by a 16 year old girl and that of a famed Bible scholar.

In an email to me, Amelia wrote …

"Dear Gerry,

" … I'm 16 years old. My mom is a Christian, and my dad may not be; I'm not really sure.

"My whole life I have been taught of this 'eternal hell' that Jesus is saving me from, and it honestly has been the single biggest stumbling block in my entire faith. I could not grasp the fact that God loved me so much but was completely okay with my dad suffering in hell forever. I would lie awake at night in tears because I was so afraid of hell and that the people I love, and possibly myself, could be going to hell. I was so unsettled by this fact that I would get so scared I couldn't even talk to God.

"About three weeks ago, I saw your book lying on our coffee table, so I took it up to my bedroom and started reading it. I was up till three in the morning reading it, and I was so amazed and infatuated by it I could not put it down!

"Never before had I ever even heard the thought that hell was not eternal, and it was the most amazing thing that I had ever read. Over the next two weeks or so, I kept reading and high-

> lighting it. I actually found myself turning off the TV and reading the book and that is a big deal because I hate to read.
>
> "Thank you SO much for writing this book. I honestly had never loved God until I read it, and now I love him so much it's crazy! This book has truly changed my life, and I'm so thankful! I feel it's a message too great to be kept a secret!
>
> "I honestly don't know how anyone can believe that God is impartial, all-knowing, loving and all-powerful if they do not believe in this Blessed Hope! It's just impossible!
>
> "Thank you so much, and I hope that this encourages you, because your book really encouraged me and changed my life forever. God bless![1]

How many millions like Amelia are suffering throughout the world? Her agony should be our agony. Something is tragically amiss in the Christian faith when children, or anyone for that matter, are left so distressed.

Listen to the grieving heart of Albert Barnes, author of the famed "Barnes' Notes":

> "In the distress and anguish of my own spirit, ... I see not one ray of light to disclose to me the reason ... why men and women must suffer to all eternity. I have never seen a particle of light ... that has given a moment's ease to my tortured mind; nor have I an explanation ... or a thought ... which would be of relief to you. ...
>
> "I confess, when I look on a world of sinners and of sufferers; upon death-beds and graveyards; upon the world of woe, filled with people who'll suffer forever; when I see my friends, my parents, my family, ... my fellow-citizens; when I look upon the whole [human] race ... and when I feel that God alone can save, and yet He does not do it, I am struck dumb. It is all dark, dark, dark to my soul, and I cannot disguise it."[2]

"It is all dark, dark, dark. ... " he says. How tragic! This compassionate man dedicated his life to serving God, but due to his mistaken view of God's character and judgments, he was blinded to the great depth and scope of God's unfailing, unending love for all people. More about Barnes.[3]

These examples are not unique. They represent millions of people who have suffered like they have. Such distress and agony are *not* the fruits of the good news of Jesus Christ.

The true Gospel ...

> Is "good tidings of great joy." (Lk 2:10)
>
> Is a "gospel of peace ... glad tidings of good things." (Rom 10:15)
>
> Causes us to "greatly rejoice ... rejoice with joy inexpressible." (1Pt 1:6, 8)

The Gospel is truly glad tidings of indescribable joy when God's character and judgments are rightly understood. It caused a 16 year old girl to say she loved God "so much it's crazy! ... it's a message too great to be kept a secret!"

Acknowledgments

I thank God for you, Denise—my wife, soul mate and best friend of 38 years. I could not have asked for a better wife, mom and grandmother for our children and grandchildren. Our deep discussions about the difficult questions of life and faith over the years have helped mature me in my faith. Thank you for your patience and perseverance with me, especially in writing this book. You are awesome! May God fill you afresh each day with His peace and joy. I love you dearly.

Thank you, my daughter, Nicole, for your patience working on the cover—and re-working it until we got it right. You have been a great help and encouragement to me. Great job!

Special thanks to my daughter, Renee, for the great effort you made on proofing, formatting, editing and your invaluable counsel. May God especially bless you and your whole family for the sacrifice you *all* made. You truly persevered, Renee—I cannot thank you enough!

I praise you, Anna (my daughter)—with your sisters, for having the courage to think for yourselves about life and faith. You are awesome role models for your children. Your lives and faith inspire me. I treasure our times together and all our conversations.

Our love and prayers go out to our daughters and our grandchildren: Elliora, Esther, Ezra, Jordan, Carter, Dora and Isla, along with their dads … that we would all rest securely in our Father's eternal love.

My sincerest thanks to everyone who has worked so hard proofing the manuscript over many months. You have been such a great help and encouragement to me. May your joy and peace in Christ abound.

Foreword

"Eternal damnation is a terrifying prospect and seems inconsistent with God's mercy, as well as disproportionate in relation to any mortal sin. Can the Bible really have threatened such a punishment? Many of the great ancient theologians thought not, and Gerry Beauchemin, in *Hope For All*, has done a real service in presenting, in clear and accessible terms, the reasons why there is hope for all."

David Konstan[4]
Prof. of Classics, NYU. Emeritus of Classics and Comparative Literature, Brown University. Co-author of *Terms for Eternity*.

"This book will very likely change the way you think about God, about people, about yourself and about human destiny. The ten anchors Gerry Beauchemin succinctly unfolds for you in this short work concern a crucial aspect of all of our lives: our concept of God. It shapes who we are and influences how we both regard and treat other people. If we think God is unjust, uncaring or cruel, then it becomes easier for us to be. But if our horizon envisions a God that is just, caring and compassionate, then we too will be so inclined. This isn't just a matter of theology or 'doctrine,' it critically affects how we live our lives here and now.

"The world-view Gerry presents in this book, and which is based upon accurate translations of key passages of the Bible, will bring you peace, joy, faith—and most importantly, will engender love within the core of your being (1John 4:19). It will transform you and liberate you from fear. Without any reservations I commend this book for your serious consideration."

Jonathan Mitchell, M.A.,
Translator of the New Testament[5]

About the Book

Hope For All presents ten broad Biblical themes or anchors each supporting God's prevailing love for all people. When all ten truths permeate your heart, an unshakable foundation for hope ensues.

My goal was to keep this book as concise and simple as possible yet detailed enough—with the endnotes, to satisfy critical minds. I recommend bookmarking the Notes section for easy referencing.

For a quick overview keep the endnotes for later. In this way you will easily grasp the core message without getting overwhelmed. These ten truths total *only 105 pages* and can be read in an evening or two.

Responses in the Questions Considered section will be easier to understand if you read all ten Anchors first.

I often abbreviate scriptures to highlight the pertinent points.

Brackets in scripture quotations provide alternative readings or author notations.

Italics are for emphasis.

Bolding of superscripts indicates additional author comments or scripture quotations.

Scripture lists are numbered when commentary is included, otherwise, bullet points are used.

Quotes are from the New King James Version unless stated otherwise.

For numerous translations and study aids: www.BibleGateway.com; www.BlueLetterBible.org [6]

Abbreviations

M - Text—Greek New Testament According to the Majority Text
NT, OT—New Testament, Old Testament
NU-Text—Nestle-Aland G NT 26th E. / United Bible Societies 3^{d} E.
H or **G** with a number: Strong's **H**ebrew or **G**reek Concordance reference number
G—Greek; **H**—Hebrew; **Lit**—literally; **GB**—author note
Bible Books: www.hbl.gcc.libguides.com/BibleAbbrevChicago

BIBLE TRANSLATIONS:

ABP (LXX), Apostolic Bible Polyglot	NABRE, New American Bible Revised
AMP, Amplified Bible	NAS, New American Standard
ASV, American Standard Version	NCV, New Century Version
CEB, Common English Bible	NEB, New English Bible
CEV, Contemporary English Version	NET, New English Translation
CLT, Concordant Literal Translation	NIRV, New Int'l Readers Version
CJB, Complete Jewish Bible	NIV, New International Version
DBY, Darby Translation	NLT, New Living Translation
DRA, Douay-Rheims 1899	NLV, New Living Version
DLNT, Disciples Literal NT	NKJV, New King James Version
ERV, Easy-T0-Read Version	NOAB, New Oxford Annotated Bible
ESV, English Standard Version	NOG, Names of God Bible
EXB, Expanded Bible	NRSV, New Revised Standard Version
GNT, Good News Translation	NRSVCE, NRS Anglicized Version
GW, God's Word Translation	NTAT, New Testament: A Translation
HCSB, Holman Christian Standard	OJB, Orthodox Jewish Bible
HNV, Hebrew Names Version	PME, Phillips Modern English
ISV, International Standard Version	REB, Rotherham's Emphasized Bible
JB, The Jerusalem Bible	RSV, Revised Standard Version
TNT, Jonathan Mitchell Translation	TEV, Today's English Version
KJV, King James Version	TLB, The Living Bible
LB, Living Bible	TNT, The New Testament (Mitchell)
LEB, Lexham English Bible	SNT, Source New Testament
LXX, Septuagint, Ancient G OT	VOICE, The Voice
MOUNCE, Reverse-Interlinear NT	WE, Worldwide English NT
MSG, The Message	WEB, Webster's Bible
MYLT, Modern Young's Lit. Translation	WEY, Weymouth NT in Modern Speech

Most at www.Biblegateway.com, www.BlueLetterBible.org, www.Amazon.com

Preface

I've believed in Jesus as far back as I can remember. The most difficult part of my faith in Jesus has been the Biblical warnings about endless punishment. I could never understand the "endless" part of that. Whenever I would really think about it, I would wonder if the Jesus story was even true.

How could a good God create millions of people *knowing* they would sin and then suffer forever as a result? It made no sense to me. Can you relate? Have you ever tried to imagine suffering forever? When does forever end? What's a billion years in comparison?

What if endless suffering was your ultimate fate or that of a loved one? Has this possibility ever tormented you? If so, you are among the millions of us who have suffered such agony.

Nothing dishonors God or fosters unbelief more than the horrid doctrine of endless punishment. This fact alone should cause us to question this doctrine and examine for ourselves what the Holy Scriptures *really* teach in relation to it.

After years of studying the Bible and the writings of respected Christians on this theme, I've discovered that our loving Creator and Father does *not* condemn anyone to endless pain. In all His judgments, our Father seeks only our good—through loving correction and discipline.

If you will prayerfully ponder these ten Anchors of Hope, you'll find a firm and secure basis for believing that God's love prevails in *every* life.

We have this hope as an anchor for the soul, firm and secure.[7]

ANCHOR 1

Hope in History

The story of God's prevailing love begins *before* creation—before the beginning of history. From there we will briefly examine Biblical history in relation to God's unfailing love and the teaching of endless punishment.

Before Creation

Unlike what our religious tradition has taught us, there has only been one plan—"Plan A." Our Creator got it right the first time, and nothing has taken Him by surprise, including human sin and failure. The apostles Paul, Peter and John all make that very clear in the next five statements:

- "*Grace* ... was given to us in Christ Jesus *before time began.*" (2Tm 1:9; Eph 1:4-5)
- "Redeemed ... with the precious blood of Christ ... *foreordained before the foundation of the world.*" (1Pt 1:18-20)
- "Jesus was the Lamb slain *from the foundation of the world.*" (Rv 13:8)
- "The hidden wisdom of God ... *predestined* to be for our glory *before the ages began.*" (1Cor 2:7-8 JB)
- "The mystery ... from the *beginning of the ages* has been hidden ... accomplished in Christ." (Eph 3:9-11)

The mission of Jesus to save all humanity has always been part of God's plan, and that fact should bring us great peace and comfort. We are safe and secure in the loving arms of our heavenly Father.

Old Testament Silence

The startling thing is that the Old Testament (OT), which spans over 4,000 years—that's 2/3 of Biblical history, does *not* mention or teach about a place of endless punishment![8] Certainly, if endless pain threatened all humanity, a loving God would have warned the world about it from the very beginning. But He did not!

Not only is endless pain *not* taught in the OT, but instead we find words of great hope and joy! Let's take a brief look at its earliest stories and statements:

Genesis 1

> "God saw *everything* He had made [past, present and future] and *indeed* it was very good!" (Gn 1:31)

God could not have said this knowing that billions of people were destined for endless suffering. He knows the future[9] and would have known our horrific fate before creating us! Everything would not have been indeed very good but indeed indescribably horrendous.

Genesis 2

At the very beginning, *not* 4,000 years later, God warned our first parents of the consequences of sin in Genesis chapter two. He called it death.[10] Death is not a code word for endless life in pain. And note: death is *not* the last word with God (Anchor 5).

Genesis 3

After humanity's first sin, God immediately prophesied Jesus' total victory over evil on our behalf.[11] Instead of condemning Adam and Eve (with all humanity) to endless pain, He extended mercy by clothing them in tunics of skin.[12] This was a prophetic sign of our Savior's death for us.[13] Just think! In judging our first sin, God gave us profound hope!

Genesis 4

Note how God dealt with Cain, the first murderer. This would have been an ideal time to warn of endless punishment. But instead, He had mercy on him by protecting him.[14] Not only was endless penalty *not* declared, mercy was extended.

Genesis 5-11

Consider the great flood of Noah's time. Death was not God's final answer for those who drowned! Christ Himself went and preached the Good News specifically to them![15]

The Gospel to Abraham

Here is one of the greatest promises in the Bible—made to Abraham, the patriarch of Israel. It is repeated *seven* times in Scripture in various forms. The number seven signifies completeness and perfection.[16]

> "In you *all* the *families* of the earth shall be *blessed*." (Gn 12:3; 18:18; 22:18; 26:4; 28:14; Acts 3:25-26; Gal 3:8)

Paul called *this* the Gospel (Good News) and acknowledged that we are justified by faith! Observe:

> "Scripture, foreseeing that God would *justify* the Gentiles by *faith*, preached the *gospel* to Abraham beforehand, saying, 'In you *all* the nations shall be *blessed.*'" (Gal 3:8)

The key question is this: Do "nations" include every person on earth? The apostle Peter says "Yes!"

> "In your seed *all* the families of the earth *shall be* blessed. To you *first*, [not exclusively] God, having raised up His Servant Jesus, sent Him to bless you, in turning away *every one of you* from your iniquities." (Acts 3:25-26)

Note the words *every one of you*. Everyone is destined to be blessed.[17] That is good news of great joy for all people!

Agony of Love

But I have a question: How are any of us blessed if we are tormented in mind and heart over the threat of endless suffering after we die? I'm thinking of my wife, daughters, parents, grandkids and everyone I love, including myself. Unless I believe that *all* my loved ones will share in the joys of heaven with me, joy is impossible—only anguish is left. It can't be otherwise if we truly love others a*s* we love ourselves, which is the true life of Christ.

Tragically, there's a dark side of a particular Christian theology, which teaches a distorted and horrific vision of God.[18] One of its early American proponents preached these shocking words:

> "The sight of Hell's torments will exalt the happiness of the saints forever. ... Can the believing husband in Heaven be happy with his unbelieving wife in Hell? Can the believing father in Heaven be happy with his unbelieving children in Hell? Can the loving wife in Heaven be happy with her unbelieving husband in Hell? I tell you, yea! Such will be *their sense of justice* that it will increase rather than diminish their bliss."[19]

I'm deeply grieved ... especially in light of this man's horrific description of hell.[20] How does a person become so heartless? Jesus explains it in the following analogy:

Lamp of the Body

The lens through which we interpret the Scriptures is our perception (our "eye") of God's nature and character—particularly His love and its scope.

> "The lamp of the body is the eye. If therefore your eye is good [or sound[21]], your whole body will be full of light. But if your eye is *bad* [not sound, diseased, unhealthy],[22] your whole body will be full of darkness.
>
> "If therefore the light that is in you is darkness, how great is that darkness!" "Take heed that the light which is in you is *not* darkness." (Mt 6:22-23; Lk 11:34-36)

Other passages confirm that a "bad eye" is a misapprehension of God's goodness stemming from an unsound or sick (selfish) heart.[23] It distorts our moral compass, or even worse, reverses its polarity:

> "Woe to those who call evil good and good evil, ... put darkness for light and light for darkness, ... bitter for sweet and sweet for bitter, ... who are wise in their *own eyes*!" (Is 5:20-21)

This is very serious because it skews how we interpret the Scriptures relative to God's love, mercy, grace, justice and judgment. We end up believing evil things about God, thinking they are actually "good." Tragically, this theology is still shared by many today.[24]

"Tweet" from God

Have you ever received a hand-written note, a text message or a "tweet" from God? You would say "Of course not!" But in fact you have—if you own a Bible. The Ten Commandments were engraved by God Himself on tablets of stone.

> "Written with the finger of God." (Dt 9:10)[25]

The God of the universe wrote humanity a personal note! Billions of people hold the Ten Commandments in the highest regard.

The Bible contains over 783,000 words and will take the average Bible reader one to three years to read. Most Christians have not read it cover to cover. But how long does it take to read the Ten Commandments? Two minutes! Compared to the Bible, it's a mere tweet. Here's my point: If something as horrific as endless punishment loomed over all humanity, surely God would have warned of it on these crucial tablets. But He didn't. However, He did *warn* us of two limited penalties!

> "*Visiting* the *iniquity* of the fathers ... to the third and fourth generations[26] of those who hate Me, but showing mercy to thousands [of generations[27]]. ... For the Lord will *not hold* him *guiltless* who takes His name in vain." (Ex 20:5-7)

Although *visiting iniquity* and *not holding guiltless* provide no specific details about these penalties, they do reveal two critical points that are conclusive to my thesis: The judgment of those hating God has a defined limit: several generations—the opposite of endless punishment. Furthermore, *mercy to thousands* of generations is hyperbole meaning that God's mercy *never ends*. That harmonizes perfectly with what God said elsewhere to Moses in this same context:

> "'Cut two tablets of stone like the first ones, and I will write on these tablets the words that were on the first tablets which you broke. ... [I am] merciful and gracious, longsuffering, and abounding in goodness and truth, keeping *mercy for thousands* [of generations—i.e., forever[28]], forgiving iniquity and transgression and sin, by no means clearing the guilty ... to the third and the fourth generation.'" (Ex 34:1, 6-7)

Amazing! God's stone tablets, written with His *finger*, known the world over, proclaim His limited judgment and infinite mercy!

The Torah

Jewish researcher Ariela Pelaia writes:

> "In answer to the question, 'What happens after we die?' the Torah,[29] our most important religious text, is surprisingly silent. Nowhere does it discuss the afterlife in detail. When the ancient rabbis talk about *Gehenna* [translated hell in the New Testament], the question they are trying to answer is 'How will bad people be dealt with in the afterlife?'
>
> "Accordingly, they saw *Gehenna* as a place of punishment for those who lead an immoral life. However, the time a person's soul could spend in *Gehenna* was limited to twelve months and the rabbis maintained that even at the very Gates of *Gehenna* a person could repent and avoid punishment.[30] After being punished in *Gehenna* a soul was considered pure enough to enter Gan [Garden of] Eden."[31]

Proclamations of Hope

There are many promises in the Old Testament that affirm God's prevailing love and mercy for all.

For example, Psalm 136:1-26:

> 1 "Oh, give thanks to the Lord, for He is good! For His mercy endures forever.
> 2 "Oh, give thanks to the God of gods! For His mercy endures forever.
> 3 "Oh, give thanks to the Lord of lords! For His mercy endures forever.
> 4 "To Him who alone does great wonders, For His mercy endures forever.
> 5 "To Him who by wisdom made the heavens, For His mercy endures forever.
> 26 "Oh, give thanks to the God of heaven! For His mercy endures forever."

All 26 verses of Psalm 136 end in the same way. In fact, "For His mercy endures forever" is seen 42 times in the Old Testament!

Note God's *all-encompassing* love and mercy in the following OT examples. I have summarized them for clarity:

- All the families of the earth shall be blessed. (Gn 12:3, 28:14)
- All the nations of the earth shall be blessed. (Gn 18:18, 22:18, 26:4)
- All the ends of the world shall turn to the Lord. (Ps 22:27a)
- All the families of the nations shall worship before God. (Ps 22:27b)
- All those who go down to the dust shall bow before God. (Ps 22:29)
- All flesh will come to God. He provides atonement. (Ps 65:2-3)
- All kings shall fall down before God. (Ps 72:11a)
- All nations (peoples) shall serve Him. (Ps 72:11b)

- All nations shall come, worship and glorify God—a God full of compassion, and gracious, long-suffering and abundant in mercy. (Ps 86: 9, 15)
- All the kings of the earth shall praise Him when they hear the words of His mouth. (Ps 138:4)
- All He has made will receive His compassion. (Ps 145:9b NIV)
- All will experience the Lord's goodness because He is gracious and full of compassion, slow to anger and great in mercy. (Ps 145:9a, 8)
- All God's works are wrapped in His tender mercies. (Ps 145:9b)
- All God's works shall praise Him. (Ps 145:10)
- All living things will have their desires satisfied by His open hand. (Ps 145:14-16)
- All people will receive a feast from God. (Is 25: 6)
- All people and nations will have the covering and the veil that was cast over them destroyed. (Is 25: 6-7)
- All faces shall have their tears wiped away as God swallows up death forever. (Is 25:8)
- All mankind together will see the glory of God. (Is 40:5 NIV)
- All the ends of the earth shall see the salvation of God. (Is 52:10)
- All nations, at *that* time, will gather to honor the Lord no longer following their stubborn evil hearts. (Jer 3:17 NIV)
- All nations and peoples of every language worshiped Him. (Dn 7:14 NIV)
- All people will have God's Spirit poured out on them. (Joel 2:28 NIV)
- All peoples' lips will be purified that they may call on the LORD and serve him shoulder to shoulder. (Zep 3:9 NIV)

The above, though not exhaustive, strongly affirm God's unfailing, unending love for all people. And King David would add: "Great is Your mercy ... You have delivered my soul from the depths of *Sheol* [translated "hell" 31 times in KJV; "*Hades*" in LXX [32]]." (Ps 86:13)

Just think ...

God's mercy and love *will* prevail—even in *Sheol!*

The Early Church

Consider this startling fact: Belief in endless punishment was *not* the predominant view of the Christian world during its first 500 years when Jesus' followers read the Scriptures in the original Greek! Dr. Edward Beecher writes:

> "Augustine himself wrote, 'Some, nay rather, multitudes, do not believe in the eternal punishment of the condemned' (Enchirid., 112). ... Deoderlein says, 'In proportion as any one was eminent in learning in Christian antiquity, the more did he cherish and defend the hope of the termination of future torments.' (Theol., ii., 199) ... Thus it appears, by applying penetrating tests to history, that the modern orthodox views as to the doctrine of eternal punishment, as opposed to final restoration, were not fully developed and established till the middle of the sixth century, and that, then, they were not established by thorough argument, but by imperial authority."[33]

I recommend Beecher's, *History of Opinions on the Scriptural Doctrine of Retribution*. It presents a concise historical exposition on what the early church believed about ultimate human destiny. It is available as a free download.[34]

For more on the Early Church, see note.[35]

If Endless Punishment Threatened All People ...

- God would *not* have thought everything was *good*.
- He would *not* have called it "death."
- He would *not* have waited 4,000 years to warn us.
- He would have engraved it in stone for *all* to see.
- All families and nations would *not* be blessed.
- God's mercy would *not* endure forever.
- God's precious promises would be meaningless.

I remind you, God has planned our redemption from before creation! Furthermore, the fact that the Old Testament does *not* teach endless punishment should cause us all to seriously reconsider what the New Testament really says about judgment.

*God's promises and actions in Biblical history demonstrate His prevailing love for **all** people.*

ANCHOR 2

Hope in Fire

The terms linked to the idea of "hell" in the Bible are often associated with fire. Tragically, this has incited great fear and anxiety in human hearts. But as we examine the Scriptures more closely about the nature of that fire, a whole new image of God's fire comes to light.

Three questions must be answered concerning "hell fire." Is it literal? Is it endless? Is it without purpose? The evidence I have found says "no" to all three.

Fire is Metaphorical

The word fire in "hell fire" (G *Gehenna fire*) is clearly a metaphor. For example, note the one time that *Gehenna* is used by someone other than Jesus:

> "The tongue ... is set on fire by hell [*Gehenna*]." (Jas 3:6)

Are tongues really set on fire? Do they burn in flames? No. This is metaphorical, merely underlining the seriousness of the offense.

Most Bible readers understand that when Jesus says, "unless we *hate* our parents we cannot be His disciples,"[36] He is speaking metaphorically. Why should fire be any different?

In referring to the judgment of "hell" (G *Hades*), Jesus said:

> "Capernaum will be brought down to hell [*Hades*]."
> (Mt 11:23 KJV)

Clearly, a city that is "brought down" to *Hades* is metaphorical; cities do not literally go to *Hades*. More on *Hades* in Anchor 4.

Scholars Testify

R.V.G. Tasker, general editor of the Tyndale New Testament Commentaries, says:

> "It is difficult to overestimate the emotional and spiritual damage ... when fire is understood literally!"[37]

Thomas Allin, author of *Christ Triumphant*, wrote:

> "The whole Bible is oriental. Every line breathes the spirit of the east, with its hyperbole and metaphors, and what to us seem utter exaggerations. If such language be taken literally, its whole meaning is lost. When the sacred writers want to describe the dusky redness of a lunar eclipse, they say the moon is *turned into blood*. He who perverts Scripture is not the man who reduces this sacred poetry to its true meaning. Nay, that man perverts the Bible who hardens into dogmas the glowing metaphors of eastern poetry—such conduct Lange calls 'a moral scandal.'"

Allin continues:

> "So with our Lord's words: Am I to hate my father and mother or pluck out my right eye literally? Or take a case by Farrar: 'Egypt is said to have been an iron furnace to the Jews[38] and yet they said, "it was well with us there," and sighed for its enjoyments.'[39] Therefore I maintain that no doctrine of endless pain can be based on eastern imagery, on metaphors mistranslated very often, and always misinterpreted."[40]

Dr. Rocco Errico, a scholar of Aramaic, the language which Jesus spoke, writes:

> "An Aramaic speaker's purpose was not to deliver the message in scientifically accurate terms: He piles up his metaphors and superlatives, reinforced by a theatrical display of gestures and facial expression in order to make the hearer feel his meaning. He speaks as it were in pictures. ... It is also because he loves to speak in pictures and to subordinate literal accuracy to the total impression

of an utterance, that he makes such extensive use of figurative language. ... He is fond of metaphor, exaggeration and positiveness in speech. To him mild accuracy is weakness."[41]

Dr. Boyd Purcell writes:

"This understanding of the Aramaic language and culture [Errico's quote] explains exactly why Jesus used all these vividly strong picture words in general and especially in regard to hell. ... He needed to communicate in the manner His audience would have readily understood. If Jesus had spoken in a mild manner, He may have lost his audience."[42]

My friend and Bible teacher John Gavazonni wrote:

"Every passage of scripture [mis] used as a proof-text for endless punishment, is in pictorial, metaphorical, symbolic language, filled with hyperbole. ... Coming from a Mediterranean ethnicity, growing up watching my Italian parents, grandparents, aunts and uncles expressing themselves in a way very similar to the Hebraic manner, I've had an advantage of getting the *feel* of what our Lord Jesus and his apostles were really conveying by their very vivid, dramatic style of communication. It's good to be reminded that it would have been expected that Jesus would have spoken with very animated gestures, as is second nature to us Italians. There's the old joke: Cut off one of the fingers of an Italian, and he loses 1/10 of his vocabulary."[43]

Bible scholar William Barclay said:

"It was the eastern custom to use language in the most vivid possible way. Eastern language is always as vivid as the human mind can make it."[44]

Jesus illustrated Barclay's statement when He said to Peter:

"Get behind Me, *Satan*; ... you are not mindful of the things of God." (Mk 8:33)

Was Peter really Satan?

To the Pharisees, Jesus said:

> "Blind guides, who strain out a gnat and swallow a camel ... whitewashed tombs ... full of dead men's bones ... Serpents, brood of vipers!" (Mt 23-33)

Were the Pharisees tombs and serpents who swallowed camels?

Jesus spoke constantly using metaphors and allegory:

> "All these things Jesus spoke to the multitude in parables; and without a parable He did not speak to them." (Mt 13-34) [45]

Fire is Purposeful

Bible "fire," whether metaphorical or literal, is a vivid and graphic term meant to capture our attention. It emphasizes *both* the gravity and transforming nature of God's acts and judgments. Because Bible fire is so grossly misunderstood as something shocking and horrendous, I list numerous examples from Scripture that show the positive and purposeful side of that fire. Consider these examples:

- God spoke to Moses through a *flame of fire*. (Ex 3:2-4)
- He led Israel by a *pillar of fire*. (Ex 13:21)
- *Temple fires* burned continually making atonement. (Lv 6:12-13; 1:4, 13; 2:2, 9; etc.)
- God gave *His law in fire*. (Dt 5:22, 9:10; 33:2)
- He answered Gideon, David, Elijah and Elisha *by fire*. (Jgs 6:21; 1Chr 21:26; 1Kgs 18:24; 2Kgs 2:11; 6:17)
- God was worshiped for His eternal mercy when *His fire* consumed the sacrifices. (2Chr 7:1-3)
- The Lord washes away filth by the *spirit of* judgment and *burning*. (Is 4:4)
- The Lord protects His people with *flaming fire* (a defense of divine love and protection—AMP). (Is 4:5)
- A *burning coal* touched Isaiah's mouth and his iniquity was taken away ... sin purged. (Is 6:5-7 NAS)

- God is *the devouring fire ... everlasting burning* with whom the righteous dwell.[46] (Is 33:14-15)
- We are *not burned walking in fire, nor scorched by its flame.* (Is 43:2)
- We are *refined; tested in the furnace of affliction.* (Is 48:10)
- God's Word *burns* in our hearts. (Jer 20:9; Lk 24:32)
- His Word is *like a fire.* (Jer 23:29)
- His throne is *a flaming fire* with wheels *burning with fire.* (Dn 7:9)
- A *river of fire* flows from before Him. (Dn 7:10 NAS)
- All the earth is devoured with *God's jealous fire and then restored.* (Zep 3:8-9)
- The Lord is a *wall of fire* around Jerusalem, her glory. (Zec 2:5)
- He is like *a refiner's fire ... will purify.* (Mal 3:2-3)
- Christ *baptizes with fire.* (Mt 3:11)
- Jesus longs to *send fire* on the earth. (Lk 12:47-49)
- The Holy Spirit *descends in fire.* (Acts 2:3)
- Fire *tries everyone's work.* "Everyone"! (1Cor 3:13)
- We are *saved "as through fire."* (1Cor 3:15)
- God's ministers are *a flame of fire.* (Heb 1:7; Ps 104:4)
- God Himself is *a consuming fire*—without consuming our being. (Heb 12:29; Mal 3:6)
- Faith is *tested by fire.* (1Pt 1:7)
- *Fiery trials* are cause to rejoice. (1Pt 4:12-13)
- *Fire exposes everything* or all the deeds done on earth, i.e., makes truth known. (2Pt 3:10b EXB[47])
- Christ's eyes are *a flame of fire,* His countenance like the sun. (Rv 1:14, 16)
- God's *refining fire* is an expression of His love—a "chastening," bringing true riches. (Rv 3:17-19)
- The seven *lamps of fire* are the spirits of God. (Rv 4:5)
- The judgment of the "lake of fire" is in the (assuring) *presence* of the Lamb—Jesus. (Rv 14:10)[48]
- There is a sea of glass and *fire in heaven.* (Rv 15:2)

Can you see how prevalent and purposeful Bible fire is? Think what fire does! It transforms matter from one form to another—a perfect metaphor for God's transforming work in our lives! And though at times we see fire in destructive contexts, it does not impede a good purpose in the larger scheme as seen in Anchor 5. God's purposes and designs for His children and all creation will prevail as seen in Anchors 8 and 9.

Fire Transforms

What does fire have to do with God?

> "God is *love*." (1Jn 4:8, 16)

> "God *is* a *consuming fire*." (Heb 12:29)

Therefore, God is a loving, consuming fire. And what does God's love consume? Our Sin—i.e., our selfishness, evil thoughts and tendencies, our pride—anything impure. So then, a "consuming" fire is a "purifying" fire—a fire which transforms us. It expresses itself in many ways.

Fire Refines

The prophet Malachi said something profound about God's consuming, purifying nature:

> "He is like a refiner's fire and like launderers' *soap*. He will sit as a refiner and a *purifier* of silver; He will *purify* the sons of Levi [priests who represented the people before God], and *purge* them as gold and silver, that they may offer to the Lord an offering in *righteousness*. Then the offering of Judah and Jerusalem [i.e., "all" the people] will be pleasant to the Lord. ... And I will come near you for judgment. ... For I am the Lord, I do not change [love never ends[49]] therefore you are *not consumed* O sons of Jacob [nation of Israel]."[50]

God's "fire" does not "consume" or annihilate our being, but purifies our nature. In refining His priests, God was refining the nation whom they represented—a people called Israel. The people of Israel were given a unique task to bless all families of the earth through Christ.[51]

Fire Washes

> "The Lord has *washed away the filth* of the daughters of Zion ... by the spirit of judgment and by the spirit of *burning*, then the Lord will create above *every* dwelling place of Mount Zion ... a *flaming fire* by night." (Is 4:4-5)

"Daughters of Zion" is a metaphor for Israel and the loving, caring, patient relationship God has with His chosen-for-a-purpose people.[52] God's judgment fire washes the "filth," e.g., the selfish ways and motives from all of us. Note the all-inclusive phrase: *every dwelling*.

Fire Devours

> "All the earth shall be devoured with fire *that* they *all* may call on and serve the Lord." (Zep 3:8-9)

Being *devoured with fire* is for the express purpose of bringing all people to seek and to serve God.

Fire Prompts Worship

> "*All the earth* shall *worship* You and *sing praises* to You. ... He is awesome in His doing toward the sons of men. ... Oh, bless our God, you peoples. ... *For* You, O God, have tested us; You have *refined* [purified-EXB] us as silver is refined. ... We *went through fire* and through water." (Ps 66:4-12a)

All the earth (everyone) will worship and sing praises to God because no one is excluded from His purifying fire. Note the word *For* which links worship and praises with His refining fire. But you might be thinking, "How can we know this includes 'hell'-fire [*Gehenna* fire]?" The following verse reveals it:

Fire Purifies All

> "*Hell fire* [G *Gehenna* fire] ... is not quenched. *For everyone* will be seasoned [purified-GNT][53] with *fire*." (Mk 9:47-49)

This is a revealing passage! Note the word *For* which links *Gehenna fire* with a *purifying* fire that affects *everyone*![54] This direct association is unmistakable. Since "everyone" will experience this fire (at least to some degree), "hell fire" cannot be endless. Think about it for a moment. Furthermore, the word *never* in "shall *never* be quenched" (Mk 9:43) is not part of the Greek text.[55]

Fire Brings Rich Fulfillment

> "You laid *affliction* on our backs. ... We went through *fire*. ... But you brought us out to *rich fulfillment*." (Ps 66:11b-12)

The afflictions of life with all their trials, sorrows and hardships, referred metaphorically as *fire*, serve a wonderful purpose. They bring *rich fulfillment!*

Because God loves us, He brings us through afflictions. That's how He molds us or transforms us into His image—as seen most clearly in Jesus Christ.[56] Can anything be more fulfilling than this?

Love Burns Like a Blazing Fire

> "*Love* is as strong as death, its jealousy [ardor][57] unyielding as the grave [severe as *Sheol*–NAS]. It [love[58]] *burns* like *blazing fire*, like a *mighty flame*. Many waters *cannot quench love*, rivers cannot wash it away." (Sg 8:6-7 NIV)

God's love for us all is relentless, unyielding, unquenchable ... burns like a blazing fire—a mighty flame ... rivers cannot quench His fiery love or wash it away. Death and *Sheol* are no barrier to His love.

> *"Where can I go from Your Spirit?*
> *Or where can I flee from Your presence?*
> *If I ascend into heaven, You are there;*
> *If I make my bed in hell*[59] *behold, You are there.*
> *If I take the wings of the morning,*
> *And dwell in the uttermost parts of the sea,*
> *Even there Your hand shall lead me,*
> *And Your right hand shall hold me."*[60]

It matters not what kind of fire we must face, whether it's a …

- burning coal …
- flaming fire …
- refining fire …
- consuming fire …
- devouring fire …
- unquenched fire …
- baptism of fire …
- spirit of burning …
- furnace of fire …
- testing fire …
- lamp of fire …
- river of fire …
- lake of fire …
- mighty flame …
- blazing fire of love …

Fire conforms us to the character of our loving Father, who loves us too much to leave us in our sins.[61]

This single truth assures us that *Gehenna fire* cannot be literal, endless and without purpose.

God's loving and consuming fires
transform us into His image.

ANCHOR 3

Hope in Judgment

Does God have a remedial and corrective purpose in His judgments or are they solely punitive? As we have seen in Anchor 2, they are remedial even when it may not be immediately obvious. Scripture assures us of this, since God does *not* change.[62] If His past and present judgments have been just and purposeful, we can rest assured that His future ones will be too.

Examples of Remedial Purpose

Observe God's good purposes in the following examples. Note what is italicized:

1) "When Your judgments are in the earth, the inhabitants of the world will *learn righteousness.*" (Is 26:9)

2) "You have appointed them for judgment. ... You have marked them for *correction.*" (Hab 1:12)

Judgment teaches righteousness, bringing correction!

3) "*Happy* is the man whom God *corrects*; Therefore do not despise [His] chastening. ... " (Jb 5:17)

God's chastening corrects us, bringing happiness.

4) "For He bruises, but He binds up; He wounds, but His hands *make whole.*" (Jb 5:18)

Judgment hurts—bruises and wounds are involved, but it makes us whole!

5) "In trouble they *visited You*, they poured out a *prayer* when Your chastening was upon them." (Is 26:16)

God's chastening draws us closer to Him and moves us to pray.

6) "Before I was afflicted I went astray, but *now I keep Your word.*" (Ps 119:67)

7) "It is *good for me* that I have been afflicted, *that I may learn* Your [demands, requirements—EXB]" (Ps 119:71)

God's affliction is a *good* thing—it teaches us His requirements and values and leads us to keep His word.

8) "The Lord will scatter you. ... But from there you will *seek the Lord.*" (Dt 4:27-29)

9) "When you are in *distress* and all these things have come upon you [from being scattered], in the latter days you will *return to the Lord* ... and *listen to His voice. For* the Lord ... is a *compassionate* God; He will *not* fail you." (Dt 4:30-31 NAS)

What motivates God in judgment? Compassion! His goal? Our reconciliation and obedience. He won't fail us!

10) "I have driven them in My anger. ... I will bring them back ... for the *good* of them." (Jer 32:37-39)

Our Father desires our *good* even in His "anger." Separation in judgment is *not* endless; He brings us back!

11) "Through deceit they refuse to know Me. ... Therefore ... I will *refine* them and try them." (Jer 9:6-7)

Even if we *refuse* or reject God, He will refine (purify) us! Sin is *not* God's defeat, but His opportunity.

12) "The Lord has *washed away the filth* ... by the spirit of judgment and ... burning." (Is 4:4)

God's *burning* judgments wash away our filth.

Nothing Stops God—Not Even Satan!

13) "[They] were delivered to Satan that they may *learn* not to blaspheme." (1Tm 1:19b-20)

14) "Deliver such a one to Satan for the destruction of the flesh, that his spirit may be *saved.*" (1Cor 5:5)

This makes total sense, since our heavenly Father is GOD. He will teach us and save us through any means He chooses. No power in all the universe can subvert God's power to accomplish His will in us (Anchor 8).

Hope for the Nations

15) "He will proclaim judgment to the nations ... *until* he should issue his judgment[63] *victoriously.* And in his name the nations *shall have hope.*" (Mt 12:18-21 NTAT)

The evidence is overwhelming: God's judgments are for our correction and transformation. And since they always have purpose, we can rest assured that they will culminate in victory!

There is hope for all!

The Perfect Parent

Since we, as human beings, created in God's image,[64] naturally discipline our children for their good, it is only normal to expect the same from God our Father. Jesus Himself used this kind of reasoning:

> "If you ... know how to give good gifts to your children, how much more will your Father." (Mt 7:11)

So it is right to compare human parenting with God's.

Observe:

16) "God *chastens* and *corrects you*, for His punishment is *proof of His love*. Just as a father punishes a son he delights in *to make him better*, so the Lord *corrects* you." (Prv 3:11-12 TLB)

17) "When we are judged, we are *chastened* [child-*trained, educated* and disciplined[65]] by the Lord." (1Cor 11:32)

18) "[God] *chastens* us for our *profit*, that we may be partakers of His holiness. ... *Afterward* it yields the peaceable *fruit of righteousness* to those who have been *trained* by it." (Heb 12:10-11)

I recall when our daughters were young, Denise and I had to discipline them at times, but it was always for their good and with love, never as pay-back. And today, as mature adults, they are the same way with their children. We are merely reflecting the nature of our heavenly Father. And since God is the Father of all people (Anchor 7), we are further assured that His judgments are purposeful for everyone, even those considered unbelievers.[66]

Synergy of Judgment with Mercy

There is a critical dynamic about God's judgments that few of us understand. In fact, it powerfully validates God's good purpose in all His judgments. King David seems to have known this, and its truth made him sing for joy:

> "I will *sing of mercy **and** judgment*: unto Thee, O Lord, will I *sing*." (Ps 101:1 KJV)

David could sing because he knew God's judgments worked with His mercy to accomplish His will in our lives. However, we have been taught to see mercy and judgment as opponents instead of partners in God's plan. But on closer observation, we see them as complementing elements of our Father's love. They work hand in hand to accomplish one goal—reconciliation between Father and child.

Let us observe a few passages that bear this out. Note what I have italicized:

1) "To You ... belongs mercy; *for* You render to each according to his work." (Ps 62:12)

Mercy, in this case, is expressed in God's just recompense. Note the word "for."

2) God visits His sons' transgressions with the rod and stripes. "*Nevertheless*, My loving-kindness [mercy] I will not utterly take from him." (Ps 89:30-34)

Mercy follows punishment.

3) "Lord ... you were to Israel a forgiving God, though you punished their misdeeds." (Ps 99:8 NIV)

Even though God forgave them, He still disciplined them.

4) "Her iniquity is pardoned; [yet] she has received from the Lord ... *double* for all her sins." (Is 40:2)

Pardoned sins *still* incur consequences. And whatever may be the reason for the word *double* here, the point is that *double* indicates something with a defined limit. It is *not* infinite.

5) "With a little wrath I hid My face from you for a moment, *but* with everlasting kindness I will have mercy on you, says the Lord, your Redeemer." (Is 54:8)

Momentary wrath is followed by everlasting kindness.

6) "Christ forgave you. ... *But* he who does wrong will be repaid, ... and there is no partiality." (Col 3:13, 25)

Though forgiven, we still incur consequences for doing wrong. That's because our Father disciplines us for good.

7) Though He utterly destroys, [yet] through repentance forgives. (Dt 4:24, 26, 29-31)

Utter destruction is followed by repentance and forgiveness.

8) "Say to those with fearful hearts, 'Be strong, do not fear; your God will come … with vengeance [recompense—ABP[67]]; with divine retribution [recompense—NAS] He will come to save you.'" (Is 35:4 NIV)

There's a sense in which we shouldn't fear God's recompense—because divine retribution ultimately saves (or perfects) us.

9) "Each one … [is] recompensed for his deeds [yet] He made Him … to be sin on our behalf." (2Cor 5:10, 21 NAS)

Though Christ is made sin for us, we are nonetheless recompensed for our deeds.

10) The Father … judges according to each one's work, [yet] we are redeemed. (1Pt 1:17-19)

Even though we are redeemed, we are still judged according to our works.

As you can see, God interweaves mercy with judgment.

It seems there are two dimensions to God's forgiveness; a legal or forensic one, and then a familial or relational aspect.[68] The first is based on Adam's loss and Christ's victory for us,[69] and the second, on our responses to our Father's call and commands. He invites us and expects us to follow Christ in love and good deeds, and holds us accountable to that. That is why our loving Father integrates judgment with mercy in order to achieve His good purposes in each one of us.

How We Live Has Consequences

God's judgments are an expression of His mercy, even when they seem void of it.

Think of this:

> "Judgment is without mercy to the one who has shown no mercy." (Jas 2:13)

And why? So we will learn to be merciful and be blessed as a result!

> "*Blessed* are the merciful, for they shall obtain mercy." (Mt 5:7)

When our Father's fearsome judgments are without apparent mercy to those who have shown no mercy, it is only because He must provide strong medicine to bring healing to unmerciful hearts. Yet even when our Father has to withhold mercy, He does so with a merciful intention. In some cases, tough love is the only remedy for an uncaring heart.

Interestingly enough, though our Father loves us all and desires our well being in every way, there seems to be a place for fear in His purposes—the right kind, of course. Its purpose is to teach us about love:

> "There is no fear in love; but perfect love casts out fear, because fear involves punishment [chastening—CLT] and the one who fears is not perfected in love." (1Jn 4:18 NAS)

How we live and love affects our peace of mind. As long as selfishness abides in us, fear will gnaw at us—it can't be otherwise. It all comes back to the priority of love.[70] Remember, our purpose in life is to become like Jesus—perfect in love![71] And we should rejoice because God is working in us towards that goal.[72]

Note carefully: many think that because they have "accepted" Christ, no judgment awaits them. Yet Scripture abounds with warnings to believers. For example:

> "We must *all* appear before the judgment seat of Christ, that each one may receive what is due him for the things done while in the body, whether good or bad." (2Cor 5:10 NIV)

> "He who does wrong will be repaid for what he has done, and there is no partiality." (Col 3:25)

No one escapes judgment.[73]

How we respond to suffering people affects what we will experience in judgment. We will be judged by how we have cared for the hungry, strangers, the poor, the sick, prisoners, orphans and widows.[74] Rewards and losses are at stake.[75] Some will qualify for the *first* resurrection and reign with Christ 1,000 years.[76] Others will weep with remorse *for a time*.[77] Yes, judgment and sorrow are real, and they serve a good purpose.

Rejoicing In Judgment

King David went so far as to rejoice over God's judgments!

> "He shall judge the people righteously. Let the heavens *rejoice* … the earth be *glad.*" (Ps 96:10-13 KJV)

> "Oh, let the nations be *glad* and *sing for joy*! For You shall judge the people righteously." (Ps 67:4)

> "The judgments of the Lord are … more to be desired … than gold, … *sweeter* also than honey." (Ps 19:9-10)

Justice, judgment and mercy moved David to say:

> "Justice and judgment are the habitation of thy throne: mercy and truth shall go before thy face. Blessed is the people that know the *joyful sound*: they shall walk, O Lord, in the light of thy countenance." (Ps 89:14-15 KJV)

Judgment leads to a joyful sound because of the blessing it ultimately brings!

> "*Sing* unto Him a *new song.* … He loveth righteousness and *judgment* [justice]: the earth is *full* of the *goodness* of the Lord." (Ps 33:3-5 KJV)

How can we, even for a moment, entertain the thought that such positive and joyful language about God's judgments could in any way imply everlasting punishment for anyone?

As you continue reading all ten Anchors of Hope in this book, you will come to see why David could rejoice in God's judgments like he did.

The idea of judgment no longer hinders my inner peace as I also obey Paul's exhortation to meditate on what is *noble ... just ... lovely ... of good report ... praiseworthy ...* etc.[78]

I can truly believe and rejoice in *all* of God's wonderful and comforting promises. The joy of the Lord has become my strength![79]

God's judgments serve a good purpose.

ANCHOR 4

Hope in Ancient Greek

Hell, to most Christians, is a fate of endless suffering. What can be worse? Even after billions and billions of years, it starts all over again … and again … and again. It's impossible to imagine. And some even say its fires are literal! Scores of horrid depictions about hell have been taught in Christian writings over the centuries.

However, the eternal terrors of hell conjured up in all these images have no place in the Holy Bible. Rather, they are rooted in ancient and medieval mythology.[80]

The pertinent Hebrew and Greek terms related to divine judgment are *Sheol, Hades, Gehenna, Aiōnios, Kolasis* and *Eis tous aiōnas tōn aiōnōn*. I will use the first three, not "hell," in all quotes.

Observing closely how these terms are used in Scripture will confirm the limited and purposeful nature of God's judgments.

Hebrew *Sheol*—Greek *Hades* (H7585; G86)

The KJV translates *Sheol* as "hell" 31 times and *Hades* as "hell" 10 times. However, most translations *never* translate them as "hell." *Sheol* refers to the grave or the abode of the dead."[81] The Greek Septuagint (LXX)[82] translates *Sheol* as "*Hades*." Thus these two terms are synonymous in their Biblical usage.

Let us learn the truth from the Scriptures:

1) "The Lord kills and makes alive; He brings down to *Sheol* [ABP *Hades*] and raises up." (1Sm 2:6 NAS)

2) "God will redeem my soul from the power of *Sheol* [ABP *Hades*]." (Ps 49:15 NAS)

3) "From the hand of *Hades* [83] I shall rescue them." (Hos 13:14a ABP)

How can *Sheol* and *Hades* be endless if God *raises up*, *redeems* and *rescues* us from them?

4) "Where is your sting O *Hades*?" (Hos 13:14b ABP)

These words imply that there is no sting. But if *Hades* were truly the destiny of billions of people as many teach, and its sufferings never end, its sting would be devastating.

The Apostle Paul certainly knew the meaning of *Hades*. That is why he could proclaim this next verse:

5) "O grave [*Hades*[84]] where is your victory?" (1Cor 15:55b KJV from Hos 13:14)

Hades occurs 11 times and the KJV *always* translates it hell *except* this one time! Why? The KJV translators were mandated by the King to *not* compromise Church doctrine.[85] To admit that hell is *not* victorious would have violated that mandate.

Note! This is the *only* time Paul ever used the word *Hades*.[86] Surely if he thought it meant endless punishment, he could never have made this claim. Instead he would have warned of it throughout all his letters! Make no mistake, if even one person was sentenced to infinite pain in hell—hell would be victorious![87]

6) "Capernaum ... shalt be brought down to *Hades*. ... It shall be more tolerable for the land of Sodom in the day of judgment." (Mt 11:23-24 KJV)

To say one kind of endless punishment is more tolerable than another contradicts the gravity of infinite punishment, for it is its endlessness that makes it so terrifying. But this passage makes perfect sense if both punishments are measurable—one being more severe than the other.

7) "I ... have the keys of *Hades* and of death." (Rv 1:18 KJV)

This implies Jesus will unlock the gates of *Hades* and release its captives as other passages indicate or imply.[88]

8) "Death and *Hades* delivered up the dead which were in them: and they were judged, every man according to their works." (Rv 20:13 KJV)

If *Hades* releases its dead, it cannot be endless, thus harmonizing with all God's judgments.[89]

Greek *Gehenna* (G1067)

Gehenna was a physical location—a garbage dump just outside the city of Jerusalem.[90] Nevertheless it also had a metaphorical application alluding to some form of after-life judgment.

Let us learn from the Scriptures:

1) "Whoever says, 'You fool,' shall be guilty enough to go into the fiery *Gehenna. Therefore* ... be reconciled ... make friends ... so that your opponent may not hand you over to the judge ... and you be thrown into *prison*. Truly I say to you, you will not come out of there *until* you have paid up the last cent." (Mt 5:22-26 NAS)

The word "until" means that *Gehenna's* metaphorical prison is not endless—it lasts only *until* the last cent is paid! The word "therefore" (v. 23) directly links *Gehenna* (v. 22) to the illustration that follows which concludes with this prison (v. 25). Even Jonathan Edwards[91] admitted this "prison" refers to *Gehenna*.[92]

It is important to note that this is the first time Jesus referred to *Gehenna*—thus it is most appropriate that He would specify its duration. Also it's found at the beginning of the New Testament for all to see in what is perhaps the greatest sermon ever preached, the "Sermon on the Mount"![93] Finally, Jesus reiterates this "until" warning of God's judgment two additional times, in Mt 18:34-35 and Lk 12:58-59.

2) In this same context Jesus referred to God's law of justice, as discussed in Anchor 6:

> "Do not think that I came to destroy the law. ... " (Mt 5:17-21)

> "An eye for an eye, and a tooth for a tooth." (Mt 5:38; Ex 21:24)

This fundamental "eye for eye" teaching or law, was an essential step in raising humanity to a higher plane—the law of love. It was our tutor to bring us to Christ.[94] He taught us that each crime deserves a measured penalty—a reference point on which He would expand. He unmistakably affirmed its validity in these immortal words:

> "With what judgment you judge, you will be judged; and with the measure you use, it will be measured back to you."
> (Mt 7:1-2)

Thus, the idea of endless punishment is fallacious—it is *not* measurable. It contradicts Christ's clear teaching.

3) "You make him *twice* as much a son of *Gehenna* as yourselves." (Mt 23:15)

If *Gehenna* is infinite, i.e., immeasurable, it cannot be deserved *twice* as much as another punishment. It makes sense only in the context of a defined, measured penalty.

4) "How will you ["sons of *Gehenna*" v. 15] escape the sentence of *Gehenna*? Therefore ... " (Mt 23:33; 23:15, 33, 37-39 NAS)

This implies that these will *not* escape! Yet observe how Jesus immediately showed them His love:

> "O Jerusalem, Jerusalem, the one who kills the prophets and stones those who are sent to her! How often I wanted to gather your children together, as a hen gathers her chicks under her wings, but you were not willing!" (Mt 23:37 NAS)

What affection! But now comes judgment:

> "Behold! your house is being left to you *desolate.*"
> (Mt 23:38 NAS)

Something tragic is occurring, yet this is not the end of the story!

> "*For* I say to you ... you will not see Me *until* ... "
> (Mt 23:39 NAS)

Whatever this *desolate* judgment entails, it endures only *until* something else occurs. Note the pivotal words *for* and *until.* As we saw in Matthew 5:26, God's judgment endures until its purpose is attained. Note what happens next.

> "*For* ... you will not see Me *until* you say, '*Blessed* is He who comes in the name of the Lord!'" (Mt 23:39 NAS)

These "sons of *Gehenna*"[95] in verse 15, later bless the Lord. Having petitioned for His execution, cursed Him while on the cross, they subsequently had a change of heart and repented. Desolation opened their eyes. The lesson: God's judgments transform us as we saw in Anchors 2 and 3.

5) "*Gehenna fire.* ... *For everyone* will be salted [purified][96] with fire." (Mk 9:47b, 49)

Gehenna fire purifies *everyone.*[97]

This makes perfect sense, since eventually *Gehenna* will be a holy place: "The whole valley where dead bodies and ashes are thrown [*Gehenna*], and all the terraces out to the Kidron Valley ... will be *holy* to the LORD. The city [Jerusalem] will never again be uprooted or demolished."[98] This is so fitting in light of Anchor 10!

Greek scholar David Bentley Hart, in the postscript of his New Testament, presents a comprehensive yet concise historical and Biblical essay which affirms that *Gehenna* was *not* endless.[99]

Greek *Aiōnios* (G166)

Aiōnios is translated "everlasting" and "eternal" in most Bible translations. For example:

> "These will go away into everlasting [*aiōnios*] punishment, but the righteous into eternal [*aiōnios*] life." (Mt 25:46)

This is the key text usually quoted in defense of endless punishment. But is it accurate? Not according to *The Emphasized Bible*:[100]

> "These shall go away into *age-abiding correction*, but the righteous into age-abiding life." (Mt 25:46)

Age-abiding correction is *not* everlasting punishment.

Note the judgment clause in these additional translations:

- ... *chastening eonian* (CLT).[101]
- ... *eonian pruning* (TNT).[102]
- ... *rehabilitation for a set period of time* (SNT).[103]
- ... *punishment age-during* (MYLT).[104]
- ... *aeonian punishment* (TCNT).[105]
- ... *Punishment of the Ages* (WNT).[106]
- ... *age-abiding punishment* (FAABT).[107]
- ... *age-long punishment* (2001T).[108]
- ... *chastening of that Age* (NTAT).[109]

As we see in these ten translations, Matthew 25:46 does *not* teach endless punishment. A reliable way we can verify the accuracy of these translations is to examine the Septuagint, the Greek Old Testament used by the Apostles in the time of Christ.

The Greek Old Testament—Septuagint (LXX)

The Septuagint is perhaps our most authoritative ancient document affirming the limited nature of *aiōnios* in Mt 25:46a—having itself become part of the inspired New Testament Canon. Prof. David Bently Hart says it "provides nine-tenths of all the quotations from [the OT]

Hebrew scripture found in the New Testament."[110] Scripture interprets itself!

Consider the following ten passages based on the Septuagint:[111]

- Circumcision is an *aiōnios* (*olām*) covenant
  until the New Covenant replaces the old.
  (Gn 17:13; Heb 8:6-13; 9:15)

- Mountains are *aiōnios* (*olām*)
  until they are scattered and collapse.
  (Hb 3:6; Is 40:4; Mk 13:31; 2Pt 3:10)

- Jonah was in the fish for *aiōnios* (*olām*)
  until three days later. (Jon 2:6; 1:17)

- The field of the Levites is their *aiōnios* (*olām*) possession
  until the New Covenant ends their priesthood. (Lv 25:34; Lk 16:16; Heb ch 7-9, esp. 8:1-13; 9:11-15)

- Ruins [NIV] are *aiōnios* (*olām*)
  until they are rebuilt. (Is 58:12; 61:4)

- Hills are *aiōnios* (*olām*)
  until made low and the earth burned up. (Gn 49:26; Is 40:4; Mk 13:31; 2Pt 3:10)

- An *aiōnios* (*olām*) landmark is not to be moved
  until it is lost, destroyed or otherwise disturbed. Nothing is permanently fixed in this world. (Prv 22:28; 23:10)

- A priest makes atonement as an *aiōnios* (*olām*) statute
  until the priesthood is changed. (Lv 16:32-34; Lk 16:16; Heb 7:27-28; 8:4-8; 1Jn 2:2)

- He remembered the *aiōnios* (*olām*) days
  yet those days ended. (Is 63:11)

- God's people stumbled from the *aiōnios* (*olām*) paths
  until those paths ceased or changed with the change in the law. (Jer 18:15; Heb ch 7-9)

Can you see how *aiōnios* does *not* mean "eternal" in any of these cases? These are only a sample. Professor Marvin Vincent asserts that 80% of the 150 occurrences of *aiōnios* in the Septuagint imply limited duration.[112] This is critical, since this word qualifies punishment, *Gehenna* fire, destruction and judgment.[113] No judgment, qualified by *aiōnios,* should be interpreted as endless.

Augustine and Eternal Life

Augustine, who knew little of the Greek language, *assumed* that if eternal punishment was not eternal, neither was eternal life, since both are cited in Matthew 25:46.[114] Did he make a valid point? It seems not.

❖ The Creeds Disprove Augustine

The early Church sheds critical light on this idea in its creeds. Along with the Septuagint, the ancient creeds are an important authority in determining the meaning of the Greek word *aiōnios,* normally translated "eternal" in our English Bibles.

Dr. Edward Beecher writes:

> "Two of the earliest creeds use the very words of Christ, '*aionian life*;' other creeds throw light on their sense, especially on the sense of the word *aionios*. This kind of evidence is as direct and authoritative as is possible. It is the testimony of the early Church speaking in her creeds."[115]

Note how the last clause of the Nicene Creed compares with the earlier Apostles' Creed:

Apostles' Creed:

> "I believe in the resurrection ... and the life *everlasting* [*aiōnios*]."[116]

Nicene Creed:

> "I believe in the resurrection ... and the life *of the world to come*."[117]

Beecher continues,

> "The earlier creeds introduce '*aionios*' to qualify life. The later creeds drop it, and in place of it introduce the idea 'of the world to come,' as a perfect equivalent to *aionios*. ... This change was made without controversy or protest."[118]

This is significant, as it reveals how the native Greek-speaking leaders of the early Church understood *aionios* punishment.[119]

If *aionios life* meant *life of the world to come,* then punishment is *punishment of the world to come*. The duration of each is determined by God. Life is without end while punishment lasts until it achieves God's purpose. They are both *of the world to come*. "Of the world to come" then, clearly allows for differences in duration in the same passage.

❖ Scripture Disproves Augustine

Augustine's theory is also disproved in three additional passages which, like Matthew 25:46, refer to *aionios* two times. In all three examples, *aionios* usages are *not* of equal duration:

1) A mystery is hidden for *aiōnios* but *then* made known by the *aiōnios* God. (Rom 16:25-26)[120]

A mystery revealed in the future is not eternal, even though it is revealed by the eternal God.

2) *Aiōnios* hills melt away, *yet* His ways are *aiōnios*. (Hb 3:6)[121]

Hills are not eternal, since they melt away.[122] Yet God's ways are eternal because He is eternal.

3) God's people remembered the *aiōnios* days of Moses. ... Who divided the waters before them to make for Himself an *aiōnios* name. (Is 63:11-12)[123]

The days of Moses have ended, yet God's name never ends because He is eternal.

You see, *aiōnios* is a relative term—its duration depends on its subject and context.[124] For example, Jonah said his entrapment in the great fish was *aiōnios,* yet his ordeal only lasted three days.[125]

❖ Jesus Disproves Augustine

Jesus, our supreme authority, defined *aiōnios life* not in terms of duration, but as a quality of life:

> "This is eternal [*aiōnios*] life that they may *know* you, the only true God and Jesus Christ." (Jn 17:3)

Aiōnios life, then, is life in vital union and relationship with God.

❖ Scholars Disprove Augustine

Professors David Konstan and Ilaria Ramelli write:

> "When it [*aiōnios*] is associated with life or punishment, in the Bible … it denotes their belonging to the world to come."[126]

Professor R.V.G. Tasker wrote:

> "Aiōnios is a qualitative rather than a quantitative word. *Eternal life* is the life that is characteristic of the age [*aiōn*] to come. … Similarly, 'eternal punishment' in this context indicates that lack of charity … will be punished in the age to come. There is, however, no indication as to how long that punishment will last."[127]

Professor David Bentley Hart[128] wrote:

> "In the original Greek of the New Testament, there really are only three verses that seem to threaten 'eternal punishment' for the wicked (though, in fact, none of them actually does)."[129]

Hart adds …

> "New Testament scholars as theologically diverse as Marcus Borg and N.T. Wright have suggested that translators might do well in many or most instances to render *aiōnios* as 'of the age to come.'"[130]

Dr. Heleen Keizer defines *aiōnios* as:

"time constituting the human temporal horizon." More [131].

Greek scholar, William Barclay wrote:

"The simplest way to put it is that *aiōnios* cannot be used properly of anyone but God. ... Eternal punishment is then literally that kind of remedial punishment which it befits God to give and which only God can give."[132]

Pastor and author, Peter Hiett, Mdiv. Fuller Seminary, explains:

"It seems abundantly clear that '*aion*' is a simple noun and should be translated 'age' in English. '*Aionios*' is an adjective and in English there is no adjective that corresponds to the English noun 'age'. ... It means 'of the age.' But that leaves us with a question: 'Of what age?' In Scripture there appears to be a fundamental distinction between 'this age (or these ages)' and 'the age to come,' God's age. So fundamentally, something '*aionios*,' is something of God's age." More.[133]

Greek *Kolasis* (G2851)

William Barclay, on the word *punishment*, adds:

"I think it is true to say that in all Greek secular literature, *kolasis* is never used of anything but remedial punishment."[134]

Thayer's Greek Lexicon defines *kolasis* as:

"correction, punishment and penalty."[135]

David Bentley Hart, translates *kolasis* as *chastening*. He adds:

"The only other use of the noun in the New Testament is in 1 John 4:18 where it refers not to retributive punishment, but to the suffering experienced by someone who is subject to fear because not yet perfected in charity."[136]

The TNT defines *kolasis* as:

> "pruning (a curtailment; a checking; restraint; a lopping off—thus, a correction.)" (Mt 25:46 TNT)

It is important to realize that even if *kolasis* is translated as "punishment," it does not rule out a corrective purpose.[137]

Greek *Eis Tous Aiōnas Tōn Aiōnōn* (G—1519, 165, 165)

The Greek, *eis tous aiōnas tōn aiōnōn*, often translated "forever and ever," literally means "unto the ages of the ages."[138] Like *aiōnios*, this phrase also implies eternal when it modifies that which in itself *is* eternal—such as God.[139] Yet there are times, however, when it does *not*. Let's look at three in Revelation.

❖ Book of Revelation

> "Jesus ... *ruler* of kings on earth ... to him[140] be glory and *dominion* [*to the ages of the ages*—[141]]." (Rv 1:5-6 ESV)

Jesus reigns *to the ages of the ages*, yet His reign ends when He hands over the kingdom to His Father. He reigns "until" He has put all His enemies under His feet.[142]

> "His servants shall serve Him, ... and they shall reign [*to the ages of the ages* [143]]." (Rv 22:3-5)

Compare this to Rv 20:4, 6 which twice specifies that Christ's servants will reign with Him 1000 years—which is *not* forever.[144]

> "The kings of the earth ... [will] *see* the *smoke* of her burning, standing at a distance ... saying, 'Alas, alas, that great city Babylon, that mighty city! For in *one hour* your judgment has come.'" (Rv 18:8-10) "For in *one hour* such great riches came to nothing. ... They *saw* the *smoke* of her burning, saying, 'What is like this great city?' ... For in *one hour* she is made desolate.'" (Rv 18:17-19) "For true and *righteous are His judgments*. ... Her *smoke rises up forever and ever* [to the ages of the ages—MYLT]." (Rv 19:1-3)

This judgment is especially noteworthy for five reasons:

1. It was a *righteous* (just) judgment.
2. It was temporal, lasting *one* hour—*not* endless. This is stated three times emphasizing its importance.
3. Its purpose was *not* to annihilate individual souls.[145]
4. Its smoking aftermath ended shortly thereafter, maybe within hours or days—again, *not* endless. Only the record of this event lives on as a warning to subsequent generations.
5. It indicates that the similar *smoke* of the lake of fire[146] torments (rising "*for ages of ages*"[147]) is also *not* endless.[148] Why would it be? Nothing here contradicts God's true and righteous judgments as established throughout Scripture.[149]

The above three passages affirm the limited nature of the phrase "*to the ages of the ages.*"[150]

Scripture Interprets Scripture

❖ A Superlative

Ages of the ages seems to be one of many superlative phrases.

For example:

- *Song of songs* (Sg 1:1)
- *Vanity of vanities* (Eccl 12:8)
- *Servant of servants* (Gn 9:25)
- *God of gods* (Dt 10:17)
- *Prince of princes* (Dn 8:25)
- *Holy of holies* (Ex 26:33 NAS)
- *Hebrew of Hebrews* (Phil 3:5)
- *King of kings* (1Tm 6:15)
- *Lord of lords* (1Tm 6:15)

All of these phrases raise one object above others in their class. It seems only right that *ages of the ages* would have a similar connotation, referring to the most momentous and climactic ages among all others.[151] Christ initiated His rule in the *church age* and will continue to expand it in the *millennial age* and beyond.

❖ Paul Testifies

The Apostle Paul spoke of the *ages* (plural) to come:

> "God ... made us sit together in the heavenly places in Christ Jesus, that in the *ages to come* He might show [exhibit; display; demonstrate[152]] the exceeding riches of His grace in His kindness toward us in Christ." (Eph 2:6)

To whom will God demonstrate His grace in future ages? To those in greatest need—those outside the Holy City's gates.[153]

Ancient Greek does not teach endless punishment.

ANCHOR 5

Hope in Death

According to our Christian tradition, it does not matter if we live 5 or 105 years, death ends all possibility of salvation. But why? What is it about our last breath that seals our eternal destiny? Would God impose such an arbitrary and unfair limitation? I don't think so.

Consider the unborn, babies, young children and the mentally handicapped who die? Do you think there's absolutely no hope for them—that they are all suffering in judgment forever? Of course not.

So then, since we believe God's mercy extends to these four groups of human beings—who all come to faith after death, how can we say everyone else has no hope? How fair is that to the rest of us? Isn't God fair? Think about it ... Where does the Bible say death ends *all* hope of salvation? The verse most quoted in support of that idea reads:

> "Each person is destined to die once and after that comes judgment." (Heb 9:27 NLT)

How does this statement deny hope after death? All it says is that judgment follows death. It says nothing about what follows judgment. As we saw in Anchors 2 and 3, judgment is full of hope and purpose.

Let us observe what the Scriptures say concerning the hope of salvation beyond this life:

Hope in Death

1) "He [God] will *swallow up* death. ... " (Is 25:8)

2) Christ *abolished* death. (2Tm 1:10)

3) "The last enemy that will be *destroyed* is death." (1Cor 15:26)

4) *"There shall be no more death. ... "* (Rv 21:4)

5) Jesus destroys the one who had the *power of death.* (Heb 2:14)

Since death is swallowed up, abolished, destroyed, is no more, and conquered by Christ's power, it can neither impede nor prevent God from saving anyone—ever. No one can remain dead if death is abolished. It is not the act of "dying" that really matters, but its *aftermath.* If even one person was held in death's grip forever, death would always exist—an enemy *never* abolished or destroyed, and would possess eternal power—power that only God wields!

6) "For if their [Israel] being *cast away* is the *reconciling of the world*, what will their acceptance be but *life from the dead.*" (Rom 11:15)

"Life from the dead," in view of the world's reconciliation, affirms great hope for all.

7) "He is not the God of the dead but of the living for all live to Him." (Lk 20:38)

Because the dead ultimately live to God, there must be hope in death, unless there is no hope in God Himself.

8) "Certainly we must die ... like water spilled ... that cannot [in the natural] be gathered up again. *But* God[154] does not take away life; instead he devises ways for the banished to be restored." (2Sm 14:14 NET)

We as human beings are helpless in overcoming death, *but* God is not.

9) "God ... gives life to the dead." (Rom 4:17)

10) Jesus holds the keys of death. He is the same yesterday, today and forever. (Rv 1:17; Heb 13:8)

Think about who Jesus is: His name means *Savior*.[155] He is the Good Shepherd who came to seek and to save the lost[156] ... who seeks *until* He finds. ... [157] He never changes! In every age, as long as there are lost sheep, He rescues! To hold *death's keys* implies that He will use them to release death's captives.[158]

11) New Testament believers must have had hope for salvation in death, since some were baptized *for* the dead:

> "What will they do who are baptized for the dead, if the dead do not rise at all? Why then are they baptized for the dead?" (1 Cor 15:29)

Greek scholar, William Barclay explains that Paul "merely asks if there can be any point in it if there is no resurrection and the dead never rise again."[159]

The fact that this was a New Testament practice further confirms to me that there's hope for salvation *beyond* this short life.

12) Jesus affirmed the forgiveness of *every* sin in the resurrection age ... except one.[160]

The fact that any sins at all are forgiven after death confirms that death is no barrier to salvation. And take note, the resurrection age is *not* the final age![161]

13) Christ died that He might be Lord of *both* the dead and the living. (Rom 14:9)

Lordship over those who have died affirms hope in death, for we must remember who our Lord is: the Savior of the world—a Savior who doesn't change![162]

14) "Christ ... suffered ... the just for the unjust that He might bring us to God, being put to death in the flesh but made alive by the Spirit, by whom also He went and preached to the spirits in *prison*, who formerly were disobedient, when once the *Divine long-suffering waited* in the days of Noah." (1 Pt 3:18-20)[163]

Recall the meaning of this word "prison." It's the same metaphor Jesus used for the *Gehenna* judgment[164] which we saw endures only *until* it achieves its Divine purpose. With that in mind, note this well known hermeneutic: "If the plain sense makes sense, seek no other sense."[165]

The question is, from what vantage point do Peter's words make sense? They are an enigma to those who think death bars all hope of future salvation, but make perfect sense if we believe death is no barrier for God.

Greek scholar, William Barclay wrote:

> "If Christ descended into *Hades* and preached there, there is no corner of the universe into which the message of grace has not come. ... [Justin Martyr[166] says] 'The Lord remembered his dead ... and came down to them to tell them the good news of salvation.' The doctrine of the descent into *Hades* conserves the precious truth that no one who ever lived is left without a sight of Christ and without the offer of the salvation of God."[167]

15) In this *same context* Peter concludes his thought with this parallel and confirming conclusion:

> "They will give account to Him who is ready to judge the living and the dead. *For* the gospel has for this purpose been preached *even* to those who are dead, that though they are judged in the flesh as men, they may live in the spirit according to the will of God. ... " (1Pt 4:5-6 NAS)

Verse 5 refers to the judgment of those still alive as well as those who have physically died. The word "For" links verse 5 with 6 confirming that "death" in verse 6 is also physical. According to Barclay, there can be little doubt this passage refers to "all the dead." He says "In some ways this is one of the most wonderful verses in the Bible." More.[168]

How tragic that we've ignored, even denied such plain and comforting words because we thought death was hopeless. Opinions are extremely strong on this matter, so much so that translators have actually doctored the text to make it agree with their hopeless view of death.[169]

Pastor Heath Bradley, in *Flames of Love*, explains:

"A very large branch of church tradition, going back to the beginning of the church ... has concluded from these texts that the author is making an affirmation of the rescuing power of Christ to reach even into the depths of hell."[170]

But, you might think, "Why did Christ preach only to those of Noah's time [1 Pt 3:19] and to no one else?" Bradley adds,

"The generation of Noah came to be regarded in ancient biblical tradition as the most wicked generation ever with no chance of finding redemption. ... Peter seems to be affirming that there is absolutely no group of people outside the scope of God's will to save. If there is hope for them, there is hope for everyone!"[171]

In addition, the Ancient Creeds of the early church show the great influence this passage had on them, particularly in this clause:

"He [Jesus] descended into hell [*Hades*]."[172]

Regarding this clause, Bradley explains:

"For much of church history, this was seen as an affirmation of the all-encompassing nature of Christ's victory over the forces of evil and sin. Not even in hell are people outside the rescuing and saving power of Christ."[173]

William Barclay concludes with these insightful words:

"It may well be that we ought to think of this [Peter's words] as a picture painted in terms of poetry rather than a doctrine stated in terms of theology." More.[174]

16) Christ "led captivity [death itself] captive ... descended into the *lower parts of the earth* ... that He might fill [complete, fulfill] all things." (Eph 4:8-10; Ps 68:18-20)

Death is a prison.[175] And since Christ led the captivity of death captive, death's grip is forever broken! Jesus descended into the lower parts of the earth (*Hades*) fulfilling His mission.[176] What a confirmation of Peter's words of hope! As Paul would say,

"O death where is your sting, O *Hades* ["hell" in all other KJV occurances] where is your victory?" (1Cor 15:55)

17) Death is swallowed up in victory. (1Cor 15:54; Is 25:8)

18) Death has *no* sting. (1Cor 15:55; Hos 13:14)

If even one person is tormented forever after death, death is *not* led captive, swallowed in victory or without sting.

19) Why is hope in death so hard to embrace when God is not willing that *any* perish? (2Pt 3:9)

20) A grain of wheat dies; but then it produces much grain. (Jn 12:24)

21) What is sown is not made alive unless it dies. (1Cor 15:36)

Death then, is a necessary prerequisite in order to bring forth new forms of life!

22) Death (of our self-will) frees us from sin. (Rom 6:7)[177] What a fruitful consequence!

23-30) Recall the eight hope-filled passages under *Sheol* and *Hades* in Anchor 4.

Hope in Destruction

Destruction and death in Scripture are often used interchangeably. In this study we will consider them separately, though sometimes they overlap. *Destruction,* like *death,* does not necessarily mean permanent annihilation but can be a prerequisite for change. Consider the following:

1) "God ... *calls into being* what does not [or no longer] exist." (Rom 4:17b JB)

Even *if* destruction were the end of existence, God will call the "destroyed" back into being as He promised.[178]

2) "[God] destroys the blameless *and* the wicked." (Jb 9:22)

Destruction of the wicked cannot mean annihilation, since it also happens to the blameless as well.[179]

3) "The righteous will perish [G *apollumi* ABP LXX G622]." (Is 57:1) Yet we know they will live![180]

4) "You [Israel] shall surely perish [*apollumi*—as above]." (Dt 30:18) Yet we know that "*all* Israel shall be saved."[181]

Destruction (*apollumi*) then, cannot be a hopeless fate!

5) God brings back the "destroyed" of Sodom, Samaria and Jerusalem:

> "And your sister Sodom … and her daughters shall be *restored* as they were from the beginning."(Ez 16:55 ABP)

It makes sense that the "destroyed" are restored, since Sodom suffered the "justice" of eternal (*aionios*) fire—a fire that went out centuries ago.[182] Also, the word "justice" assures us that the fire is limited and measured.[183]

6) Egypt, though destroyed, will be healed and will return to the Lord and serve Him. (Ez 32:2-10; Is 19:22-24)

7) The peoples of Moab, Ammon and Elam are destroyed … yet the Lord brings back their captives.[184]

8) The *restoration of all things* means that whatever is "destroyed" must eventually be restored. (Acts 3:21)

9) Clay in the Potter's hand is *remade* as it pleases the Potter.[185]

For something to be *remade* it must first, in a sense, be *unmade,* i.e., destroyed.

10) Wineskins are "marred" (*apollumi*). (Mk 2:22 KJV)

11) Oil is "wasted" (*apōleia*[186]). (Mk 14:4 KJV)

These objects were not annihilated but worn and broken down.

12) "Concerning the faith [they] have suffered shipwreck, of whom are Hymenaeus and Alexander, whom I delivered to Satan [which results in the *destruction* of the flesh as seen next] that they may *learn* not to blaspheme." (1Tm 1:19-20)

These two people shipwrecked their faith and were delivered to Satan. Yet note what resulted: they *learned*, i.e., were corrected.

13) "Deliver such a one to Satan for the *destruction* [G3639] of the flesh, *that* his spirit may be *saved*. ... " (1Cor 5:4-5)

A sinner is delivered to Satan for the *destruction* of his flesh. Why? To save his spirit. Destruction, in this case, led to salvation.[187] God even uses Satan to accomplish His will to save us.

Scripture Interprets Itself

Often the first statement in a passage is defined by those which follow. For example:

14) "I will destroy [*apollumi*] the wisdom of the wise, and the cleverness of the clever I will *set aside*." (1Cor 1:19 NAS)

"Destroy" here means to set aside.

15) "Do not destroy [*apollumi*] with your food him for whom Christ died. ... Do not 'tear down' [NAS] the work of God. ... It is good neither to eat meat ... nor do anything by which your brother 'stumbles' or is 'offended' or is 'made weak.'" (Rom 14:15, 20-21)

"Destroy" here means to "tear down," cause to "stumble," "offend" and "make weak." This is *not* annihilation!

W. E. Vine states:

> "*Apollumi* (G622) is not extinction but ruin; loss, not of being, but of well being."[188]

Such ruin and loss of well being are confirmed in the previous and following passages.

16) "Because of your knowledge shall the weak brother perish [*apollumi*] for whom Christ died?" (1Cor 8:11)

No mortal can annihilate another by knowledge or anything else—especially because Christ died for all. Often *apollumi* merely means physical death.

17) "Do not work for food that spoils [*apollumi*]." (Jn 6:27 NIV)

Spoiled food decomposes, enriches the soil for a future crop. It is not annihilated, but transformed.

18) "For as many as have sinned without law will also *perish* [*apollumi*] without law, *and* as many as have sinned in the law will be *judged* by the law." (Rom 2:12)

Contrasting these scenarios reveals that *perish* cannot be annihilation, since everyone experiences judgment with its *measured* consequences.[189]

19) Think of what the cross of Jesus means: In order to "save" our life (make of it something worthwhile), we must first lose (*apollumi*) or deny it.[190] We must "die" to our self-centered life and live for God. This is not annihilation of our being but of our selfish nature. Only in dying to self do we truly live and bear fruit to God.[191]

20) Did God not say: "I kill [i.e., destroy] *and* I make alive; I wound *and* I heal?" (Dt 32:39; 1Sm 2:6)

Even in death and destruction, God will not be defeated—His promises to restore all will be fulfilled. For more: see *Hope Beyond Hell* chapter one: www.hopeforallfellowship.com/download-hope-beyond-hell/

"The Yet Factor"

There is always hope in God. This is revealed through other seemingly "unchangeable" scenarios:

21) Israel's afflictions are incurable, ... yet the Lord restores health and heals her wounds. (Jer 30:12, 17)

22) Samaria's wounds are incurable, ... yet He brings them back and restores them. (Mic 1:9; Ez 16:53)

23) Egypt and Elam will rise no more, ... yet He brings back their captives. (Jer 25:27; 49:39; Ez 29:14)

Even when things seem hopeless, there remains an unspoken factor—"the yet factor." Yet God intervenes! He always reserves the right to alter a previous course.

24) I repeat this here to highlight its relationship to destruction. "Certainly we must die ... like water spilled ... that cannot be gathered up again [i.e., it was destroyed]. But [yet] God does not take away life; instead *he devises ways* for the banished [destroyed] to be restored." (2Sm 14:14 NET)

Death and destruction are not beyond God's power to restore.

Testimony of Christ

25) The very ones Christ came to save are the so-called "destroyed" ones: "For the Son of Man has come to seek and to save that which was lost [*apollumi*]." (Lk 19:10)

Apollumi is the very condition qualifying us for salvation, so it cannot be hopeless!

26) *Apollumi* refers to the "lost" sheep that must be sought after and rescued! (Lk 15:4-6)

27) *Apollumi* refers to the "lost" son who was lost and dead but then was found and made alive again! (Lk 15:24)

28) *Apollumi* refers to the "lost" (not yet found) sheep of Israel of whom all will be saved (i.e., found).[192]

So, the lost (*apollumi*) are not those eternally destroyed, but those *not yet* found! At what point then, does *apollumi* become permanent, impeding God's power and will to save?

29) "God is able to raise up children to Abraham from theses stones." "If these should keep silent, the stones would immediately cry out." (Lk 3:8; 19:37-40)

No form of destruction can limit God, who is *able* to turn stones into His children and His worshipers.

Israel and the Prophets

30) In addition to all of the examples above, recall Israel's long history, which for centuries was a continuous cycle of judgment, destruction and restoration. What an awesome testimony of God's unfailing love for His chosen-for-a-purpose and often-rebellious people![193]

God's Total Victory

What can possibly keep God's love, mercy and grace from us?

Who or what is more powerful than God?

> "For I am persuaded that *neither death* [which includes destruction] nor life, nor angels nor principalities nor powers, nor things present nor things to come, nor height nor depth, nor any other created thing, shall be able to separate us from the love of God which is in Christ Jesus our Lord." (Rom 8:38-39)

*Nothing can separate us from God's love and mercy—
not death, not destruction, not Gehenna. ... Nothing!*

ANCHOR 6

Hope in Justice

Does God's justice *assure* hope for all? I think that once you see how God's justice relates to His holiness, His law, Jesus' death and His pleasure (as our Father), you will come away feeling very assured that there is *indeed* hope for all in God's justice.

"[Jesus] sends forth justice to victory." (Mt 12:20)

How many of us understand the great significance of this promise? I would think not many do, since so many Christians have claimed that all sin is committed against an *infinite* and holy God, and thus deserves *infinite* punishment on that basis. But is that correct? Is it Biblical? Famed colonial preacher, Jonathan Edwards, devoted over 1700 words asserting this claim. But he did so without once quoting Scripture.[194]

I say unreservedly that God's justice *is* victorious in every sense—that justice for sin is *not* endless punishment, and I base this exclusively on Scripture!

Justice and God's Holiness

Justice, in view of God's holiness, does *not* support endless punishment, whether directly or indirectly.

Consider these examples:

1) "Sing praise to the Lord. ... Give thanks at the remembrance of His *Holy* Name. *For* His anger is *but* for a moment." (Ps 30:4-5)

Note the word "For." God's holiness is the very point why His anger is *but* for a moment, not endless.

2) "I will vindicate the *holiness* of My great name ... which you have profaned in their midst. *Then* the nations will know that I am the Lord ... when I *prove Myself holy* among you in their sight. *For* I will ... *cleanse* you from *all* your filthiness and ... idols ... give you a *new heart* and ... spirit ... and *cause* you to walk in My statutes." (Ez 36:23-27 NAS)

Note the word "For." God's holiness is vindicated precisely by the display of His transforming love towards sinners, the opposite of abandonment in endless misery.

3) "O Lord my God, my *Holy* One ... You have appointed them for *judgment*; O Rock, You have marked them for *correction*." (Hb 1:12)

When a holy God executes judgment, it's for a holy purpose—our correction, thus it cannot be endless.

4) "Behold [Jesus], a gluttonous man and a drunkard, a *friend* of tax collectors and sinners!" (Mt 11:19 NAS)

Jesus, a "*Holy* Servant and *Holy* High Priest,"[195] is the radiance of God's glory, the exact representation of His nature.[196] To see Jesus *is* to see the Father.[197] And what was Jesus known for? He was a friend of sinners, even to His last breath—dying between two criminals![198] Can you picture it?

God's holiness, rather than banishing sinners from Himself forever, is at home in their presence. This makes great sense because God not only sees us as we are right now as sinners, but as we are destined to become in Christ.[199] What a contrast between God's true holiness and the distortions of human tradition!

5) "My heart recoils within me; my *compassion grows warm and tender*. I will *not* execute my fierce anger; I will *not* again destroy Ephraim; for I am God and no mortal, the *Holy* One in your midst, and I will *not* come in wrath." (Hos 11:8-9 NRSV)

Pastor Heath Bradley writes,

> "It is highly significant that the reason God gives for his compassion and refusal to come in wrath is precisely because he is 'the Holy One' who is far different from mere mortals. Far from God's holiness requiring that God punish people eternally, Hosea affirms that God's holiness is actually what compels God to refrain from wrath and to have mercy. What makes God holy or different from human beings is that God has the capacity to transcend revenge and offer mercy."[200]

6) "Great and marvelous are Your works, Lord God Almighty; just and true are Your ways, O King. ... Who shall not fear You, O Lord, and glorify Your name? *For* You alone are *holy. For all nations shall ... worship* before You, *for Your judgments* [acts of justice[201]] have been manifested."[202] (Rv 15:3-4)

Note the words "for." A holy God is being worshiped by all nations because of His just judgments. If His judgment was endless torment for most of humanity, all people would *not* worship Him for it and say "great and marvelous are Your works; ... just and true are Your ways."

Jeremiah made these remarkable statements:

7) "The anger [wrath] of the Lord will not turn back *until* He has executed and performed the thoughts of His heart. In the latter days you will understand it *perfectly.*" (Jer 23:20)

8) "The *fierce anger* [wrath] of the Lord will not return *until* He has done it, and *until* He has performed the intents of His heart. In the latter days you will consider it." (Jer 30:24)

The fact that Jeremiah repeats this statement underlines its gravity. Whatever a Holy God's fierce anger leads Him to do in justice, endures only *until* it serves the purposes of His loving heart, thus is *not* endless!

9) "Be perfect just as your Father is perfect [His holiness is integral to His perfection]." (Mt 5:38-48)

Bradley adds,

> "Jesus portrayed God's holiness, in relation to sinners, not as wrath and retributive justice, but as compassion and love. When He tells us to be 'perfect' as His Father is perfect it follows His command to love our enemies as God loves His."[203]

Luke reads (note the word "for"):

> "Love your *enemies* ... and you will be children of [like a child of] the Most High; *for* He is kind to the ungrateful and the *wicked*. Be compassionate just as your Father is *compassionate*."
> (Lk 6:35-36)

God's character [holiness] is defined as His kindness and compassion to His enemies and the wicked.

10) "For My thoughts are not your thoughts. ... My ways [are] higher than your ways." (Is 55:8)

Many defenders of endless punishment insist that we have no right to impose our human understanding on what divine justice should be. But ironically, that's exactly what people do when quoting this passage.

Isaiah 55:8 is constantly quoted in an attempt to justify God's infliction of endless punishment. But there's a problem with this. Everyone is *mis*quoting it!

Observe:

> "Let the wicked ... return to the Lord, and He will have *mercy* on him ... *for* He will *abundantly pardon. For* My thoughts are not your thoughts." (Is 55:7-8)

Note the words "for." God is higher—greater in holiness than humans are because He is greater in mercy, *not* cruelty! In misquoting this passage, they are implying the opposite about God's nature! There is no cruelty in Him whose essence is love.[204] Love defines God's holiness and sets Him apart morally from human beings.

Justice and God's Law

Since all crimes are violations of God's holy law, it makes sense that the law itself would help us understand the essence of God's justice. Let us explore two aspects of God's law—His written and His unwritten law.

The Written Law

Justice, as it is revealed in God's written law, radically opposes the idea of endless punishment. The Apostle Paul wrote:

> "The law was our tutor to bring us to Christ." (Gal 3:24)

The law is also our tutor to teach us justice.

1) "I would not have known sin [which would include injustice] except through the law. ... The law is *holy* and the commandment *holy* and *just* and good." (Rom 7:7, 12)

God's holy law is "just." But what does that mean? Let's start by examining the law as it pertains to the crime of violence. God instructed Moses, as the judge of Israel, with these words:

2) "He shall surely be punished, ... and he shall pay ... life for life, eye for eye, tooth for tooth, hand for hand, foot for foot, burn for burn, wound for wound, stripe for stripe." (Ex 21:22-24)

This is the *Lex Talionis,* the oldest law in the world. In ancient times, vengeance for a single crime was inflicted upon a whole village and far exceeded the crime committed. So, as excessive as that might seem, the *Lex Talionis* introduced mercy and a truer sense of justice when the world needed it most.

In Jewish society, the *Lex Talionis* was a civil law, not a personal mandate, and was never literally carried out by the courts—only monetarily.[205] Jesus made it clear that the *Lex Talionis* was the law for society and not for individuals—for our law is love.[206] He did not deny the "justice" of this law but affirmed it.[207]

"Do not think that I came to destroy the law [what is fair and just]. ... For assuredly I say to you, till heaven and earth pass away, one jot ... will by no means pass from the law till *all* is fulfilled." (Mt 5:17-18)

Moses decreed further:

3) "If there is a dispute between men, and they come to court ... if the wicked man deserves to be beaten ... [it will be] *according to* his guilt, with a *certain number* of blows. *Forty* ... and *no more*." (Dt 25:3)

This is precise, limited judgment! Whenever God exercises any form of judgment, it is *always* measured in proportion to the crime committed.

Jesus expressly affirmed the lawfulness of measured judgment:

4) "With what judgment you judge, you will be judged. And with the *measure* you use, it will be *measured* back to you." (Mt 7:1-2)[208]

Compare this with endless punishment. What is "measurable" about infinity? And on what Biblical grounds do our finite sins merit infinite penalty as many claim?

Judgment is *always* in proportion to deeds. The evidence for this abounds in Scripture:

- "The righteous judgment of God ... will *render* to each one *according to* [in proportion to] his deeds." (Rom 2:5-6)
- "*According* to their deeds, *accordingly* He will *repay* ... He will *fully repay*." (Is 59:18)
- "I ... give to every man *according* to his ways, *according* to the fruit of his doings." (Jer 17:10)
- "I will *repay* them *according* to their deeds and *according* to the works of their own hands." (Jer 25:14)
- "You ... give everyone *according* to his ways and *according* to the fruit of his doings." (Jer 32:19)
- "Repay her *according* to her work; *according* to all she has done, do to her." (Jer 50:29)
- "Renders to each man *according* to his deeds." (Prv 24:12)

- "To you belongs mercy; for you render to each one *according* to his work." (Ps 62:12)
- "I will judge ... every one *according* to his ways." (Ez 18:30, 19-32)
- "[Judged] *according* to your ways; *according* to your deeds." (Ez 24:14)
- "Judged *according* to their ways and their deeds." (Ez 36:19)
- "Punish *according* to his ways; *according* to his deeds." (Hos 12:2)
- "*According* to our ways; *according* to our deeds He has dealt with us." (Zec 1:6)
- "The Son of Man ... will reward each *according* to his works." (Mt 16:27)
- "We must all appear before the judgment seat of Christ ... each receives *according* to what he has done, whether good or bad." (2Cor 5:10)
- "The Father ... without partiality judges *according* to each one's work." (1Pt 1:17)
- "I am He who searches the minds and hearts. And I will give to each one ... *according* to your works." (Rv 2:23)
- More examples.[209]

❖ The Lake of Fire Judgment Supports the Written Law

The lake of fire is no different than any other judgment: it is *according to works*, not endless. John emphasized this fact *three* times in the context of the lake of fire.

> "The dead were judged *according to their works* ... each one *according to his works* ... the lake of fire."[210]

> "I ... [will] give to every one *according to his work* ... Blessed are those who do His commandments, that they may ... enter through the gates into the city. But outside [in the lake of fire[211]] are ... sexually immoral and murderers and idolaters." (Rv 22:12-15)

For more on the lake of fire, see Anchor 2 and Question #26.

❖ The Law of Liability Supports the Written Law

D. Scott Reichard writes:

> "God made Himself responsible for humanity's redemption in His laws of liability. Liability is based on ownership (Ex. 21:33-4). If a person digs a pit and does not take the necessary steps to cover it, and an ox comes along (of his own free will) and falls in the pit, he or she is liable. They *must buy* the dead ox. Other liability laws which say the same thing are Deuteronomy 22:8 and Exodus 22:5-6.
>
> "Consider the Garden of Eden. Back in the garden, God dug a pit. He did not cover it up and Adam and Eve fell in. The pit was complete with a couple of temptation trees and a tempter. God was fully aware what decision they would make. Yet God did not cover the pit. He could have prevented them from sinning by not planting the trees and placing the tempter elsewhere. But God dug that pit and purposely left it uncovered. He had a plan. The plan called for humanity to fall.
>
> "By God's own liability laws, He made Himself responsible. He purposely obligated Himself to take care of the situation. He sent His Son to pay the price. All creation became subject to death through Adam's fall. God bought the dead ox and owns it. He fulfilled the terms of redemption—bought all who fell. In doing so, He fulfilled the law. This is the Good News! Christ's blood redeemed the whole world (1Jn. 2:2; 1Ti. 2:6)!"[212] More.[213]

❖ The Law of Jubilee Supports the Written Law

> "You shall consecrate the 50th year and proclaim liberty throughout all the land to *all* its inhabitants. ... " (Lv 25:10a)

This amazing law, discussed in Anchor 10, not only affirms limited judgment, but exemplifies restorative justice.

The Unwritten Law

We all, to one degree or another, possess an innate sense of right and wrong. C.S. Lewis built his case in defense of the Christian faith on this very point.[214] Conscience is mentioned 32 times in the New Testament and serves a vital role. Through it, God speaks to our hearts affirming that the idea of endless punishment is not just by any standard—human or Divine. The following examples affirm the critical role of conscience:

1) "The law *written* in their hearts, their *conscience* also bearing witness ... in the day when God will judge." (Rom 2:15-16)

2) "By manifestation of the truth commending ourselves to *every* man's *conscience* in the sight of God." (2Cor 4:2)

3) "[Jesus] gives light to *every* person coming into the world!" (Jn 1:9)

Every person has a conscience, a vital part of our being—essential in knowing justice and truth—even peace of heart.[215]

4) "The heart is deceitful above all things and desperately wicked [sick]: who can know it?" (Jer 17:9 KJV)

Tragically, our religious tradition has dismissed conscience as nearly irrelevant, due to a mistranslation of this passage. Is the human heart "wicked" as the KJV words it, or is it "sick"? "Wicked" is *not* what Jeremiah said. He said "sick" as seen in many other translations.[216]

Strong's Dictionary defines the Hebrew (*ânash*) as:

"frail, feeble or figuratively, melancholy."[217]

The Greek Septuagint[218] reads:

"The heart is deep above all else, and [so] is man, and who shall understand him?" (Jer 17: 9-10)[219]

A "deep" heart is not necessarily a "wicked" heart and the Scriptures bear this out.

Abraham, Jesus and Paul all appeal to our conscience in discerning what is right.

In Genesis, Abraham asks:

5) "Shall not the judge of all the earth do *right*?" (Gn 18:25)

This, of course, implies we know right from wrong.

Jesus asks:

6) "If you, being *evil*, *know* how to give *good* gifts to your children, how much more will your Father in heaven?" (Mt 7:11)

Jesus is appealing to our moral sense. Though we are sinners, we still know good from evil—justice from injustice.[220] This is inherent in our nature as human beings made in God's image.[221]

Paul exhorts us to …

7) "Test *all* things and hold fast to that which is *good*." (1Thes 5:21; 1Cor 10:15)

Paul assumes we all know what is good and evil. He refers to God's judgments as an example of that.[222] This exhortation, to test *all* things, especially applies to endless punishment.

Jesus asks:

8) "Why do you not even on your own initiative judge what is *right*? *For* while you are going … into prison … you will not get out of there *until* you have paid the very last cent." (Lk 12:57-59 NAS)

Would Jesus have said this if He knew we could never get out? And if He did know it, would it be right to mislead us? This text is particularly noteworthy because they are the words of Jesus Himself in the context of the *Gehenna* judgment as we saw in Anchor 4. Note how "for" links verse 57 with 58.[223] Jesus is appealing, as Paul did, to the law written in our hearts—our conscience. Are we listening? How do *you* feel about endless punishment? Have you been troubled by its sense of injustice?

Jesus said:

> "You invalidated the word of God for the sake of your tradition." (Mt 15:3, 6, 9 NAS)[224]

Have you?

Jesus *is* the living Word (*logos*) of God who lives in us.[225] What is He saying to your heart about endless punishment—in light of God's love, mercy, judgment and justice?

> "Keep [guard] your heart with all diligence, for out of it spring the issues of life." (Prv 4:23)

Justice and Jesus' Death

Justice for sin was attained by Jesus' death. For anyone to suffer forever because of their sin would disavow the truth of the following statements:

1) "I [Jesus] ... *accomplished* the work you have given Me to do." (Jn 17:4 NAS)

2) "It is *finished* [paid in full[226]]."—Jesus' last words on the cross (Jn 19:20)

What work did Jesus accomplish? What was paid in full? The salvation of the world! That is why He is called the "Savior of the world," for that is what He does and is. His mission was not merely to "offer" salvation to all, but to procure it for all![227] He indeed succeeded.

3) "[Jesus] takes away the sin of the *world.*" (Jn 1:29)

4) "He atones for the sins of the "*whole world.*" (1Jn 2:2)

5) "He gave Himself a ransom for *all* to be testified in *due time!*" (1Tm 2:6)

6) The Day of Atonement (Lev 16) prefigured the limitless scope of what Jesus' sacrifice would accomplish. It shows how atonement covered the sins of all the people apart from their involvement. This set the stage for us to understand that Jesus would cleanse all humanity from their sin.[228]

7) "The Son of God appeared for this purpose, to *destroy* the works of the devil." (1Jn 3:8 NAS)

Jesus accomplished His mission.[229] Sentencing even *one* person to endless punishment denies this fact and proves that the devil's works were *not* destroyed. That would be an outrage of justice toward Jesus— He who ransomed *all* in sacrificing Himself.

8) "He shall see of the travail of his soul [His crucifixion[230]] and shall be *satisfied*." (Is 53:11 KJV)

How could Jesus be satisfied if His death did not accomplish its full purpose? Would you be satisfied if you purchased 100 acres and the deed stated only 99? Would you say, "Close enough"? No! And neither would Jesus, the Good Shepherd who seeks His lost sheep *until* He finds them.[231] He is not satisfied with 99 out of a 100—He wants 100% of what He has redeemed. That's just!

Justice and the Father's Pleasure

Judgment (according to deeds) is an important step in our correction and transformation, as it teaches us the gravity of our sins through experiencing the same pain we have inflicted on others. Its extent, however, depends on how merciful we have been to others and the attitude of our hearts.[232]

In itself, judgment (according to deeds) cannot fully satisfy justice in this life, as it does not undo or heal the pain our sins have caused others. Christ alone can do that. He is our Comforter, Advocate, Healer, Friend, Redeemer and Lord our Savior!

Only when God's just recompense is followed with reconciliation, with God and with each other, is justice fully realized and the Father satisfied and pleased.

Paul wrote:

> "It *pleased* the Father ... to *reconcile all* things [esp. people[233]] to Himself ... having made *peace* through the *blood* of His *cross*." (Col 1:19-20)

Jesus reconciled us *all* through His *blood*. Perfect justice, for Jesus, requires the reconciliation of all. It is both our Father's good pleasure *and* His justice! Thus God's just recompense (the *Lex Talionis*) is merely the first stage in the process of attaining justice—reconciliation is its culmination. God has a timeline, not a time limit, in attaining His loving purposes for all His children.

Paul says:

> "In [Christ] we have redemption through His blood, the forgiveness of sins, according to the riches of His *grace* ... having made known to us the mystery of [God's] will, according to His *good pleasure* which He purposed ... that in the dispensation of the *fullness of the times* He might gather together in one *all* things [esp. people] in Christ ... who works all things according to the counsel of His will." (Eph 1:7-11)

God's justice begins with discipline under the watchful eye of a loving Father. It expands over time into a higher dimension of grace and mercy—encompassing *both* judgment and mercy, woven together for our good and our Father's pleasure.[234]

God's justice assures us that endless punishment is not *Biblical—loving correction and mercy are!*

ANCHOR 7

Hope in Our Father

Can God be our Creator without also being our Father? Not according to the Bible as I understand it. To think otherwise leads to a debased view of God—one oblivious to His great love for all people.

Rev. Thomas Allin says:

> "We are told God is *not* the Father of all men; He is only their Creator! What a total misapprehension these words imply. ... For what do we mean by paternity and the obligations it brings? The idea rests essentially on the communication of life to the child by the parent.
>
> "Now paternity is for us largely blind and instinctive; but Creation is Love acting freely, divinely; knowing all the consequences, assuming all the responsibility involved in the very act of creating. ...
>
> "It seems, then, very strange to seek to escape the consequences of the lesser obligation [fatherhood], by admitting one still greater [Creator]."[235]

We cannot Biblically separate God as Creator from God as Father—they are one and the same.

Ten Affirmations of Fatherhood

1) Adam

"Adam, the *son* of God." (Lk 3:38)

This is Adam's identity—as descendants of Adam, all human beings are God's children too.

2) Being Creator Assumes Fatherhood

- "Have we not all one *Father*? Has not one God *created* us?" (Mal 2:10)
- "Is He not your *Father* ... ? Has He not *made* you [Israel]?" (Dt 32:6)
- "You are our *Father* ... our *potter*; and all we are *the work of Your hand*." (Is 64:8)
- "I will be his *God* and he shall be My *son*." (Rv 21:7)
- "Let Us make [create] man in Our image, according to Our likeness." (Gn 1:26; 9:6; Col 1:15-20)

Whatever else it might mean to be created in the image of God, it at least affirms His Fatherhood. The early church fathers confirmed this in their creeds, linking God's nature as both Father and Creator:

Apostles' Creed:

> "I believe in God, the *Father* almighty, *creator* of heaven and earth."[236]

Nicene Creed:

> "We believe in one God, the *Father*, the Almighty, *maker* of heaven and earth, of *all* that is. ... "[237]

3) Firstborn Children

Moses clarified that the Hebrews are not God's only children, but His *firstborn* children!

> "Israel is My son, My *firstborn*." (Ex 4:22 – Moses)

Jesus came first to the people of Israel[238] in fulfillment of God's initial purpose to reveal Himself through Abraham and his descendants. Israel was chosen to be God's blessing to the whole world.[239] It is the same with Christ and His Church: we are called to be lights in the world, bringing the Good News of Jesus Christ to all nations.[240]

So when the Bible says:

> "*All* of you are *children* of the Most High." (Ps 82:6)

> "I bow my knees to the Father ... from whom the *whole family* in heaven and earth is named." (Eph 3:14-15)

We can all rest assured that God is our Father too.[241]

4) Our Father

The New Testament refers to God as *Father* over 230 times.[242] It was Jesus' preferred title for God. In His most famous discourse, the Sermon on the Mount, He addressed God as *Father* 17 times![243] And note the introduction to Christianity's most famous prayer:

> "*Our Father* in heaven. ... " (Mt 6:9)

Matthew concludes Jesus' famous sermon in these words:

> "The *people* were astonished ... *great multitudes* followed Him." (Mt 7:28-29, 8:1)[244]

"The people" and "great multitudes" refer to those whom Jesus addressed when referring to God as *Our Father*. This is significant! People came from the whole region: Galilee, Decapolis, Jerusalem, Judea and beyond the Jordan river.[245]

In another discourse, Jesus referred to God as *your Father* when speaking to the public:

> "Then Jesus spoke to the *multitudes* and to his disciples saying ... 'Do not call anyone on earth your father for *One is your Father* ... who is in heaven.'" (Mt 23:1, 9)

Why was addressing God as *our Father* so important to Jesus? I believe He wanted us to know who we are—children of God, and how loved and special we are to Him.

5) The Athenians

Paul affirmed that we are all God's children! When speaking to the Athenians, people of another religion, he quoted one of their own poets who said:

> "For we also are His [God's] children." (Acts 17: 28 NAS)

Paul immediately followed this quote in saying:

> "Being *then* the *children* of God ... " (Acts 17: 29 NAS)

Paul recognized these Gentiles were his brothers and sisters in God. So even those who do not *yet* know Jesus are still God's *children*.[246]

6) One God and Father

Paul also links the oneness of God with being Father of all:

> "There is ... *one* God and Father of *all*." (Eph 4:4-10; Mal 2:10)

Our Father is not the Creator of all and Father of some, but the one God and Father of all.

7) Father of Spirits

> "Be in subjection to the Father of spirits." (Heb 12:9)

"Father of spirits" excludes no one, as every person has a spirit.

8) Meaning of Adoption

Must we be adopted to become God's children? No! That is a misunderstanding of what adoption means. Adoption is mentioned by Paul five times[247] and does not carry the same meaning as it does in our culture. Adoption was an endearing term which mirrored a Roman custom which authorized one to officially represent another for legal purposes.

W. E. Vine says,

> It "involves the dignity of the relationship of believers as sons ... not a putting into the family by spiritual birth, but a putting into the position of sons."[248]

Marvin Vincent has a similar explanation:

> "'Adoption' is a setting or placing: the placing of one in the position of a son." More.[249]

Though we all are children of God, only faithful believers are adopted sons in the Biblical and Roman sense. Such sons are led by the Spirit of God. They put to death the misdeeds of the body and willingly suffer with Christ. It never meant that God was only the Father of obedient believers. This resolves the dilemma of Mt 5:44-45 and Lk 6:35-36 (NIV) where Jesus says:

> "Love your enemies ... *that* you may be *sons* of your Father."

> "Love your enemies, do good, ... and you *will be children* of the Most High ... just as your Father is merciful."

Why would He tell them to do something in order to become sons and children when he already referred to God as their Father? A correct view of adoption resolves this.

Jonathan Mitchell explains:

> "Jesus, in Matthew 5:45, is using a Hebrew idiom, 'sons of ...' as a teaching device to indicate how His followers should live. It means 'that which has the quality and character of something, or that with which a person is associated.'" More.[250]

This explains why Jesus told the Pharisees that the devil was their father. It was a figure of speech like numerous others He used. He said: "You do the *deeds* of your father ... the devil."[251] Were these Jews actual paternal sons of the devil? Of course not—they merely acted as such.[252]

Jesus frequently used metaphors and hyperbole. Matthew said: "without a parable He did not speak to them."[253] For example: "You are *Peter* and on this *rock* I will build my church ... But he turned and said to Peter, 'Get behind me *Satan!*'"[254] Was Peter a rock or Satan? The truth is, he was neither. He was "as" a rock in one context and acted "as" Satan in another. It was the same with the Pharisees. They were no more the children of the devil than Peter was Satan or a rock.

9) Owner of All

"All souls are mine." (Ez 18:4)

Although "father" is not always used in reference to God, especially in the Old Testament, it is often inferred.[255]

We all belong to God! If He lost any of us forever, it would be His eternal loss—that of a father losing his child. But God loses nothing, especially not one of His own children!

10) Forgiving, Loving Father

"If *you then, being evil*, know how to give good gifts to your children, how much more will *your Father!*" (Mt 7:11)

Imagine! Even though we are all, in some sense, "evil,"[256] Jesus still considers God our Father! Our sins, failures and even rebellion do not change who we are as His paternal children.

"O my *rebellious children, come back* to me again and *I will heal you* from your sins." (Jer 3:22 TLB; Is 55:7-9)

Our Father does not disown us because of our failures. The parable of the wayward son is a great example of this. In that story, ...

A father had two sons and one decided to take his inheritance to pursue a life of pleasure. But the day soon came when he found himself broke and distraught. Remorseful, he decided to return home, but wondered what he would say to his father. But when his father saw him coming from afar, he ran to his son, embraced him, and kissed him fervently[257]—even before his son could explain himself.[258]

What a picture of our heavenly Father! He never gives up on us, no matter how miserably we fail. Bible scholar, William Barclay wrote:

> "There is no discipline of God which does not take its source in love and is not aimed at good."[259]

How could it be otherwise, since God our Father *is* love?[260] And if we, as parents, discipline *our* kids for their good, wouldn't it make sense that our Father would also?[261] The author of Hebrews thought so:

> "My son, do not despise the chastening of the Lord, nor be discouraged when you are rebuked by Him; *for whom the Lord loves* [He loves all[262]] He *chastens*, and scourges *every* son whom He receives [He receives all].
>
> "If you endure chastening, God deals with you as with sons; for what son is there whom a father does not chasten? But if you are without chastening, of which *all have become partakers*, then you are [as] illegitimate and not sons. Furthermore, we have had human fathers who corrected us, and we paid them respect. Shall we not much more readily be in subjection to the Father of spirits and live? For they indeed for a few days chastened us as seemed best to them, but He for our profit, *that we may be partakers of His holiness*.
>
> "Now no chastening seems to be joyful for the present, but painful; nevertheless, *afterward* it yields the peaceable fruit of righteousness to those who have been *trained* by it."[263]

Our Father disciplines us *because* He loves us. Though it may not be pleasant at the time, *afterward* it yields the peaceable fruit of righteousness—ultimately becoming like Jesus.

As a dad and granddad, I can't imagine how God—our loving Father, could send *any* of His children to endless pain.

God is everyone's loving Father.

ANCHOR 8

Hope in God's Nature

Does God love *everyone*? If so, will He *always* love us? These are critical questions. Their answers will bring us either peace and joy, or distress and anguish—they affect everything.

God Loves Everyone

Knowing that God loves everyone is the only basis on which we can be assured that He loves any of us.

Note what is italicized:

- "God demonstrates His own love toward us, in that *while* we were *still* sinners, Christ died for us." (Rom 5:8)
- "Behold! the Lamb of God who *takes away* the sin of the *world!*" (Jn 1:29)
- "By this we know *love* … He laid down His life for us." (1Jn 3:16)
- "[God] *loved us* and sent his Son as an atoning sacrifice for our sins." (1Jn 4:10 NIV)
- "And *not only* for [our sins] but *also* for the sins of the *whole world.*" (1Jn 2:2 NIV)

God loves the *whole world*—everyone! He demonstrated His love for us all in the sacrifice of Jesus.

- "For God so loved the *world* … he sent his Son to save the *world.*" (Jn 3:16-17 NIV)
- "[He] gives life to the *world.*" (Jn 6:33)
- "[He gives His] flesh for the life of the *world.*" (Jn 6:51)
- "[He] came to save the *world.*" (Jn 12:47)
- "[He is] indeed … the Savior of the *world!*" (Jn 4:42)

- "[The Father sent Him] as Savior of the *world!*" (1Jn 4:14)
- "God ... reconciling the *world* to Himself." (2Cor 5:19)

"World" is mentioned 78 times by the Apostle John alone and nowhere in the entire New Testament does it merely mean "church" or "believers" or the "elect."[264] Jesus died for *every* person on earth which includes the "ungodly," "sinners," His "enemies" and the "unjust"![265] No one is excluded from redemption in Christ!

- "The Lord laid on Him the iniquity of us *all.*" (Is 53:6)
- "Christ ... died for *all.* ... " (2Cor 5:14)
- "He died for *all.*" (2Cor 5:15)
- "It pleased the Father ... to reconcile *all* things [esp. people[266]] ... through [Christ's] blood." (Col 1:19-20)
- "[Jesus] tasted death for *everyone* [i.e., "*all mankind.*" JB]." (Heb 2:9)
- "The grace of God has appeared, bringing salvation to *all* men." (Ti 2:11 NAS)
- "Jesus gave Himself a ransom for *all.*" (1Tm 2:6)

Scripture is clear—Jesus died for all humanity.

God's Essence is Love

What is especially amazing to me about God's love is this critical point: Not only does God love ... He *is* Love. Love defines Him.

"God *is* love." (1Jn 4:8, 16)

Rev. Thomas Allin wrote:

> "God is not anger, though He can be angry. God is not vengeance, though He does avenge. These are attributes, love is essence. Therefore, God is unchangeably love. In judgment He is love, in wrath He is love ... love first, and last, and without end. Love is simply the strongest thing in the universe, the most awful, the most inexorable, while the most tender."[267]

The apostle Paul said:

> "Though I have ... all knowledge ... all faith so that I could remove mountains, but have not love, I am nothing. ... Now abides faith, hope and love, but the greatest of these is love!" (1Cor 13:2, 13)

All knowledge, even faith with power to move mountains, if it lacks love, is *nothing!* And so it is with God. It was not His limitless knowledge and power that gripped Paul's heart, but His love! Nothing sets God apart (makes Him holy) more than His love.

Jesus confirms this:

> "*Love* your enemies *that* you may be *sons* of your Father ... *perfect, just as* your Father ... is perfect." (Mt 5:44-48)

Love is what defines God as "perfect" or "holy." It is His most amazing, powerful, distinguishing, heart-warming, faith-building and life-transforming trait—it is nothing less than God Himself!

God Suffers

> "Love *suffers* long ... does not seek its own ... bears all things." (1Cor 13:4-7)

Long-suffering characterizes God because ...

"God *is* love." (1Jn 4:8, 16)

The Apostle John defines love this way:

> "By this we know love, because *He laid down His life* for us [in excruciating pain on a cruel cross]." (1Jn 3:16)

The Apostle Paul defines it similarly:

> "God demonstrates *His own* love toward us ... Christ *died* for us." (Rom 5:8)

Note he said: "His *own* love"! It was God's *own* love that was demonstrated in Jesus' death on the cross. That's because Jesus and the Father are *one*. To see Jesus *is* to see the Father. The Father is *in* Jesus.[268] That is why Paul could say:

> "God was *in* Christ [i.e., on the cross[269]] reconciling the world to Himself." (2Cor 5:19)

What does all this imply?

It implies that our Father also suffered with Jesus on the cross or 2Cor 5:19 makes no sense to me—for without suffering there is no love.[270]

In addition, what greater pain can any parent endure than to witness the torture and murder of a beloved child? Since we, as human beings (created in the image of God) would be overwhelmed in pain, I cannot see how our loving Father would not also experience such anguish.

Our Father's love is the core of the Gospel …

When our Father's *extreme* love for *all humanity* is *fully* revealed to the *whole* world in the *fullness* of time, it will melt the hearts of the most hardened sinners. Every person will worship God with *all* their heart.

What can we say in response to such love?

"We love You, Father. We love You, Immanuel (i.e., *God* with us[271]—*God* on the cross)."

Unlimited Power of God's Sacrificial Love

What great news! God loves each and every one of us to the point of dying for us! But what about our evil thoughts and ways? Does God have the power and desire to change our sinful nature? Yes! The Scriptures proclaim His limitless power and love—even for His enemies! King David, a murderer and adulterer, expressed great confidence in God's love:

> "I trust in Your *unfailing* love." (Ps 13:5 NIV)

Even when we are judged by God, as David was, God's love prevails. Consider a few examples of God's prevailing love and power:

- "For men are not cast off by the Lord forever. Though He brings grief, He will show compassion, so great is His *unfailing* love. For He does not willingly bring affliction or grief to the children of men." (Lam 3:31-33 NIV)
- "The Lord ... is *long-suffering* ... [wills] that *all* should come to *repentance*." (2Pt 3:9)
- "The long-suffering of the Lord *is salvation*." (2Pt 3:15) When does our Father's *long-suffering* end, since He *is* Love and Love *never* fails or ends?[272]
- "You can do everything ... no purpose of Yours can be withheld from You." (Job 42:2)
- "The Lord ... has sworn. ... Surely, as I have thought, so it shall come to pass." (Is 14:24)
- "Whatever His soul desires, that He does." (Job 23:13b)
- "God ... does whatever He pleases." (Ps 115:3; 135:6)
- "I will do *all* my pleasure ... I will also bring it to pass. I have purposed it, I will also do it." (Is 46:10-11)

More.[273]

What is God's will, desire and pleasure? That everyone would seek Him, turn from wrong and do right.[274] But you might think, "That's wishful thinking. Surely God can't get all He desires—evil people don't change." But, no! Evil people *do* change in the fullness of God's time.

God Can Change Anyone

Remember when Jesus told His disciples it was harder for a camel to go through the eye of a needle than for a rich person to enter God's kingdom? Those were surely despairing words as seen in their reply: "Who *then* can be saved?" But note His response: "With men it is impossible, but *not* with God; for with God all things are possible." This passage is of great importance, since it is repeated numerous times.[275]

So what is Jesus saying? I think He means that we can never, in our own strength, be good enough to merit or attain salvation—which includes sharing in God's divine nature.

Jesus proved that salvation was always possible when He transformed a murderer into an apostle—perhaps the greatest apostle of all.[276] Paul was commissioned by Jesus as His chief ambassador to the nations.[277] As such, Paul wrote most of the New Testament letters. Yet he referred to himself as the "chief" of sinners.[278] Now if God can change the worst of us, who can He not change?

Consider further:

> "[God] *will* again have compassion on us, and *will* subdue [conquer[279]] our iniquities." (Mic 7:19)

Note how it's God's compassion (i.e., love) which leads Him to conquer our sin! What a wonderful thought!

As hard as it is to conceive, God *can* change anyone! How? He transforms our heart.

Observe:

- "I will give you a *new heart* and put a *new* spirit within you ... and *cause* you to walk in My statutes and you *will keep* My judgments and *do* them ... I will cleanse you from *all* your uncleanness." (Ez 36:23, 35-38)
- "All the nations shall be gathered. ... No more shall they follow ... their evil *hearts*." (Jer 3:17)
- "I will give them a *heart* to know Me ... for they shall return to Me with their whole *heart*." (Jer 24:7)
- "I will put my law in their minds, and write it on their *hearts*." (Jer 31:33-34)
- "I will give them one *heart* and one way, that they may fear Me forever." (Jer 32:39)
- "I will put My fear in their *hearts* so that they will not depart from Me." (Jer 32:40)
- "I will put my laws into their minds and *hearts*." (Heb 8:10a)

What a God! What a promise! But ... will He do it for everyone?

No Favoritism

Good news! Everyone receives a change of heart. What God does for some, He will do for all—in His "due time."[280] Why? Because our Father is impartial.

> "How true it is that God does not show favoritism."
> (Acts 10:34 NIV)[281]

It may appear as though God shows favoritism because He is not revealing Himself to everyone right now and all hearts are *not* being changed. The problem is, we're not seeing the big picture. God reveals Himself to some sooner than to others because He plans to work through them to reach all people—in the fullness of time, in the context of the ages to come.[282] Our Father carries *all* humanity in His heart.

But how can we be assured God will truly transform every single person? That seems too hard to believe.

We can believe it ... *if* we know God's promises and power. Jesus said:

> "Ye do err *not knowing the Scriptures, nor the power* of God."
> (Mt 22:29 KJV)

Have we erred in not knowing and trusting God's promises and His power to fulfill them? Consider a few more amazing promises:

- "They *all* shall know Me, from the least of them to the greatest of them." (Heb 8:10b)
- "To You *all* [people] ... will come ... You will provide atonement." (Ps 65: 2-3)
- "Make a joyful shout to God, *all* the earth ... Say to God, 'How awesome are Your works! Through the greatness of Your *power* Your enemies [that's you and me] shall submit[283] themselves to You. ...'" (Ps 66:1-3)
- "'*All* the earth [everyone!] shall worship You and sing praises to You.'" (Ps 66:4)

Truly, God is more powerful and loving—able and willing to save than we ever imagined. Is this really so hard to believe in light of His infinite power and love? No. It's just that the idea is outside our religious box—and radically so. But it *is* Biblical, and God is not confined to any box. What He wills, He does.

Free Will in God's Will

Will *all* know God? Doesn't this go against "free will"? I don't think so. We are like fish in a fish bowl, limited in choices. Only God determines our ultimate destiny. He places us in an environment that teaches us critical lessons about life. Though they take time to learn, time is on God's side. His love and patience *never* end. In fact, they prevail!

Q. H. Shinn wrote:

> "God does not save us by arbitrary force ... [He] has resources in his universe, the all conquering agencies of love, to make the unwilling soul willing! He has light enough to make the blind see, and love enough to melt the hardened heart."[284]

Loyal F. Hurley wrote:

> "Again and again, when trouble stalks our path, we turn back to the God we've despised. When our spouse dies or our children go wrong; when loss and disaster fall on us ... we will seek the God we have neglected. That is not because God coerces us, but because He brings upon us such experiences as change our attitude ... not in anger, but in love. For love is the only ultimate power that is *not* coercive."[285]

Think a moment: Can a person be held responsible for rejecting God or Christ if they did not really know who they were rejecting—not knowing God's true nature and character or the consequences of such rejection?

Philosophy professor, Thomas Talbott writes:

> "If I am ignorant of, or deceived about, the true consequences of my choices, then I am in no position to embrace those consequences freely; and if I suffer from an illusion that conceals from me the true nature of God, or the true import of union with God, then I am again in no position to reject God freely."[286]

More on free will.[287]

Remember that *nothing* is impossible with God![288] He can transform our hearts and our minds without violating our will.

> "God ... is at work within you, giving you the *will* and the *power to achieve* his purpose." (Phil 2:13 PME)

> "Now to Him who is *able* to do *exceedingly abundantly above all* that we ask or think, according to [His] *power that works* in us." (Eph 3:20)[289]

Is God really *able* to exceed our highest hopes and expectations? It all comes down to what we believe about His love, power and will. What is the breadth and depth of His love ... the extent of His power and determination to change us?[290] How far is He willing to go? What limits will you place on God?

Good News, "The Bottom Line"

I have come to this conclusion about the Christian faith: Only if we believe God loves and saves all people can we have true assurance about our own destiny and that of our loved ones. Otherwise something depends on us—we who are sinful and prone to failure.[291] This conviction is the only truth that has ever brought me peace and lasting joy. I know. ... I've lived it.

Peace, joy and security are at the heart of the Gospel of Jesus Christ.

The Apostles Peter and Paul were not exaggerating when they made these statements:

"You *greatly* rejoice ... with joy *inexpressible* and *full* of glory."
(1Pt 1:6-8)

"For I am *persuaded* that neither death nor life, nor angels nor principalities, nor powers, nor things present nor things to come, nor height nor depth, nor any other created thing [which includes *Hades*[292]], shall be able to separate us from the love of God which is in Christ Jesus our Lord." (Rom 8:38-39)

Such indescribable joy and absolute security are not possible if we are being threatened by endless punishment.

God loves every person and always will.
He has all the time and power to transform every
heart without violating anyone's will.
His *will and love prevail.*

ANCHOR 9

Hope in God's Promises

Throughout the Bible we encounter glad tidings of good things—promises that should bring great peace and joy to every heart. But sadly, most of us have failed to experience that joy due to a flawed view of God's character and judgments.

The following ten promises are clear statements of what *is* or *will be*. They are saying that every person *will* receive the stated promise, not "might" receive it. This distinction is critical. If these statements are true ... then the faith, repentance and obedience, that are needed for their ultimate fulfillment, will occur at some point in the future. And they *are* true, for God is at work in every person.[293] He completes what He begins.[294]

God's Promises Triumph Over Law

To one extent or another we are all guilty of wrong-doing or the breaking of God's law.[295] So, of course, there are consequences.[296] Yet "the law ... *cannot* annul the covenant ... that it should make the promise of no effect."[297] Human frailty and sin cannot rescind God's promises; they *will* come to pass.[298]

Ten "All" Promises to Remember

1. Jesus draws *all* to Himself. (Jn 12:32)
2. Jesus justifies us *all*. (Rom 5:18-19)
3. *All* Israel [with all people] shall be saved. (Rom 11:26)
4. God will have mercy on *all*. (Rom 11:32)
5. *All* are brought to life in Christ. (1Cor 15:22)
6. *Every* human being will worship Christ. (Phil 2:9-11)
7. *All* will be gathered together in Christ. (Eph 1:9-11)
8. *All* will be reconciled to God. (Col 1:19-20)

9. God wills to save *all* … testified in due time.(1Tm 2:3-6)
10. God is the Savior of *all* people. (1Tm 4:9-11)

1) "I, when I am lifted up from the earth, will draw *all* people to Myself." (Jn 12:32-33 ESV)

The word "draw," Greek *helkouo,* literally means "to drag."[299] *Helkouo* is not restricted by the resistance of the object being drawn. For example, the apostle Peter, having a sword, *drew* (*helkouo*) it in defense of Jesus. He also *dragged* (*helkouo*) the net of fish to land. Paul and Silas were *dragged* (*helkouo*) into the market place. Paul was *dragged* (*helkouo*) out of the temple. The rich *drag* (*helkouo*) us into court.[300] As the sword, net, Paul, Silas and the poor were not able to resist the dragging (*helkouo*) powers that overcame them, neither can anyone forever resist the power of Christ to draw them to Himself.

2) "As through one transgression there resulted condemnation to *all* people, even so through one act of righteousness there resulted justification of life to *all* people. For as through the one person's disobedience *the many* [all people] were made sinners, even so through the obedience of the One *the many* [all people] will be made righteous." (Rom 5:18-19 NAS)

Clause 1: As through one transgression there resulted condemnation to *all* people,

Clause 2: even so through one act of righteousness there resulted justification of life to *all* people.

Clause 3: For as through the one person's disobedience *the many* [all people] were made sinners,

Clause 4: even so through the obedience of the One *the many* [all people] will be made righteous.

No one denies Clause 1 refers to all people. Clause 2 follows suit. Few deny Clause 3 refers to all people. Clause 4 must also follow suit. "The many" in the last clause must refer to the same group as the previous clauses, or it would contradict them all—violating the grammar and logic of Paul's argument. The point of Clauses 3 and 4 is merely one of contrast—"**the** one" affecting "**the** many"—*particular* versus *universal*. Prof. D. B. Hart explains why the Greek in these two passages unequivocally refers to *all* human beings:[301]

The Weymouth Translation affirms this:

> "It follows then that just as the result of a single transgression is a condemnation which extends to the *whole race*, so also the result of a single decree of righteousness is a life-giving acquittal which extends to the *whole race*. For as through the disobedience of the one individual the *mass of humanity* were constituted sinners, so also through the obedience of the One the *mass of humanity* will be constituted righteous."

Paul himself confirms this in his closing statement:

> "Where sin abounded, grace abounded much more!" (Rom 5:20)

Christ's sacrifice in restoring lives is much greater than Adam's sin in destroying them. If not, then what the last Adam (Christ)[302] has accomplished in rescuing a few is "much less" not "much more" than what sin has done.

Again, the Weymouth translation, in verse 15, powerfully expresses this glorious achievement of Christ:

> "But God's free gift immeasurably outweighs the transgression. For if through the transgression of the one individual the mass of humanity have died, infinitely greater [much more] is the generosity with which God's grace, and the gift given in His grace which found expression in the one man Jesus Christ, have been bestowed on the mass of humanity." (Rom 5:15)

God's grace has been bestowed on the mass of humanity. This is an accomplished fact. As Adam impacted all humanity in a negative way, Christ impacts all humanity in a positive way. No other conclusion fits the context, grammar, logic and God's numerous "all" promises.[303]

3) "*All* Israel [along with all people] will be saved, as it is written: 'The Deliverer will come out of Zion, and He will turn away ungodliness from Jacob.'" (Rom 11:26)[304]

Israel was called to be God's channel of blessing to the whole world;[305] a matter of privilege,[306] not superiority. Since He is not partial, if God saves all Israel, He will save everyone.[307] There is no distinction between Jews and non-Jews, since all are justified by faith.[308] Peter said Israel was the *first* to be blessed which means they are *not* the only ones.[309] Moses and Jeremiah said the same.[310] God has always had *all* nations in His heart and purposes.

4) "God has imprisoned *all* men in their own disobedience *only to show* mercy *to all* mankind." (Rom 11:32 Jerusalem Bible)

New English Bible:

> "For in making *all* mankind prisoners to disobedience, God's purpose was *to show* mercy to *all* mankind."

New Life Version:

> "God has said that *all* men have broken His Law. But He *will show* loving-kindness on *all* of them."

Common English Bible:

> "God has locked up *all* people in disobedience, *in order to* have mercy on *all* of them."

I list four translations because many others use the word "might" which could veil the grandeur of this passage. Question #8 shows why "might" in those versions is not one of uncertainty.

The "alls" in this sentence encompass *all* people, not merely Israel. Bible Scholar, C.H. Dodd says it well:

> "The universal state of disobedience has been set forth in Romans 1:18-3:20. It has been shown in the present chapter [Romans 11] that this state of mankind is within the purpose of

God ... But the final aim of that purpose is a state in which God's mercy is as universally effective as sin has been. In other words, it is the will of God that all mankind shall ultimately be saved."[311]

Note: This has particular significance because this is the closing statement (with vs. 33-36) of a long three chapter discussion.

5) "*Just as all* people die in Adam, *so all* people *will be brought* to life in Christ." (1Cor 15:22 Jerusalem Bible)

"Just as all people ... so all people" means the whole human race died, the whole human race will live. Paul is reinforcing what he said above in Romans five.

"Brought to life" does not mean to resurrect in order to annihilate or torture forever. The context denies that possibility, for in what way would death be destroyed, swallowed up in victory, and its sting lost (1Cor 15:26-28, 54-55)?

"Brought to life," Greek *zōopoieō,* implies a glorious spiritual life. It occurs 12 times in the New Testament, and never once does it hint of something negative.[312]

Finally, how can Christ be considered greater than Adam if Adam's power to condemn exceeds Christ's power to save?

Again, as I quoted above, Paul would answer ...

"Where sin abounded [in Adam], grace abounded *much more* [in Christ]!" (Rom 5:20)

6) "At the name of Jesus *every* knee will bow, of those who are in heaven and on earth and under the earth, and that *every* tongue will confess that Jesus Christ is Lord, to the *glory* of God the Father." (Phil 2:9-11 NAS)

"No one can say that Jesus is Lord except by the Holy Spirit." (1Cor 12:3)

Bowing and confessing "Jesus is Lord" implies true worship, not compelled adulation. Paul links it to the Holy Spirit and to salvation. (Rom 10:9) Furthermore, it glorifies God. Only true, heart-felt worship fits this context. Also, God is not impressed with insincerity:

> "Well did Isaiah prophesy of you hypocrites, as it is written: 'This people honors Me with their lips, but their heart is far from Me. And in vain they worship Me.'" (Mk 7:6-7; Is 29:13)

> "True worshipers ... worship the Father in ... truth." (Jn 4:23-24)

Unlike earthly despots consumed by the glory of their brute power and adulation from others, our Father is infinitely above such vanity and vain glory.

I list 20 reasons why this passage refers to genuine worship, not compelled adulation.[313]

7) God's *good pleasure* "purposed ... that in the ... *fullness of the times* He might gather together in *one all* things [especially people[314]] in Christ ... who works all things according to the counsel of His will." (Eph 1:9-11)

God's purpose is to unite all people into one, in Christ. What He decrees cannot be stopped, not even by our present rebellion. In the fullness of time, God will unite every single person through repentance and faith in Jesus.[315] This is not hard to believe when we know God's true character and nature—His unending love for all, His unfailing power to change us and His irresistible will.

8) "It *pleased* the Father ... by Him [Christ] to reconcile *all* things [especially people[316]] to Himself ... having made *peace* through the *blood* of His *cross*." (Col 1:19-20)

Note: The text states "all" *not* "some." The Father's *pleasure* is to reconcile *all* people to Himself—everyone! Yet sadly, many think the reconciliation of "all things" is not about people. But what would please our loving Father more? Reconciling His wayward children to Himself, or frogs, fish and flowers which need no reconciliation?

Furthermore, this reconciliation is through the blood of Christ's cross, which Scripture declares was shed for human beings.[317] To limit the power and extent of Christ's blood to cleanse and reconcile all people, in my view, dishonors His precious blood shed for all. I do not see any limits on what the blood of Christ has achieved and on what pleases the Father, especially since this was His intention from before creation.[318]

9) "This is *good* and acceptable in the *sight* of God our Savior; who *will* [319] have *all* people to be saved, and come unto the knowledge of the truth … Jesus … gave Himself a ransom for *all*, to be testified in *due time*." (1Tm 2:3-6 KJV)

Many translations state "desires" here instead of "will" which implies that God only "wishes" to save all people but cannot. W. E. Vine defines the Greek *thelō* here as: "'to will, to wish,' implying volition and purpose, frequently a determination, is most usually rendered 'to will.'"[320] That being said, even if *thelō* were to mean "desires" in this passage, it doesn't change anything because God accomplishes *all* His desires and does whatever He pleases anyway.

"*Whatever* His soul *desires* He does." (Jb 23:13)

"God … does *whatever* He *pleases*." (Ps 115:3)

"*I am God* … I will do *all* My *pleasure* … I will also *bring it to pass*." (Is 46:9-11)

The essential point is that God is GOD; He does all His will.

Note what I have italicized in the introduction and close of our key text. Paul underlines the truth that what is good in God's sight is that in due time, all will know that His desire to save all will be fulfilled.

10) "This is a *faithful* saying and worthy of *all* acceptance. For to this end we both labor and suffer reproach, because we trust in the living

God, who is the *Savior of all men, especially* [*malista* G3122] *of those who believe. These things command and teach.*" (1Tm 4:9-11)

What a declaration! God is the Savior of all people. Sadly, most of us have not believed these words because we have misinterpreted the word "especially." We misread it as meaning "exclusively"—when there is no textual or contextual justification for it. That is not what it means.[321] Observe this comparable and revealing passage:

"Let us do good to *all* people, and *especially* [*malista*] to those … of the faith." (Gal 6:10 NAS)

Are we to do good exclusively to those of faith? Of course not. We are to do good to everyone. Yet, since those who follow Christ represent Him before the world, they need to be especially cared for—for the sake of their witness and blessing to all people, not because they are more deserving.

So then, in what way are believers "especially" saved? They are saved now, in *this* life, in the sense that they are demonstrating the character of Christ before the world, giving evidence of their salvation.[322]

Note what immediately follows:

"Be an example … in conduct, in love … that your *progress* [becoming like Christ] may be evident to all." (1Tm 4:12-15)

The fact that believers are *especially*, and not exclusively saved, affirms that in God's *due time*[323] all will come to believe.

Finally, note the powerful opening and closing clauses of this amazing statement:

"This is a *faithful* saying and *worthy of all acceptance*. … These things *command* and *teach*." (1Tm 4:9, 11)

There is only one other passage in the entire New Testament that opens this way, and it too is a most amazing statement of hope:

"This is a *faithful saying* and *worthy of all acceptance*, that Christ Jesus came into the world to save sinners." (1Tm 1:15)

Jesus came to save sinners! That means everyone.[324] These two unique and faithful sayings, which are worthy of all acceptance, are two sides of the same coin. God is the Savior of all people!

More Promises

There are scores of hope-filled promises to be discovered once our eyes and hearts are opened to the awesome truth of God's prevailing love.

In addition to the *all* promises in Anchor 1, note these from the New Testament:

- All people are to receive good tidings of great joy. (Lk 2:10)
- All flesh shall see the salvation of God. (Lk 3:6)
- All (esp. people) will be restored in the fullness of time. (Acts 3:21)
- All families (every person—v. 26) of the earth shall be blessed. (Acts 3:25-26)
- "All in all" is what God has promised to become in every person. (1Cor 15:28)
- All peoples shall be blessed *is* the Gospel. (Gal 3:8)
- All are brought salvation by God's grace. (Ti 2:11)
- All will know Him, from the least to the greatest. (Heb 8:10-12) To know Him is eternal life. (Jn 17:3)
- All nations shall come and worship before Him. (Rv 15:4)
- All things (includes everyone) will be made new ... these words are true and faithful. (Rv 21:5)

It is tragic that the doctrine of endless punishment destroys the Bible's most precious promises.

For more amazing, life-transforming promises, see "Proclamations of Hope."[325]

The Power of God's Promises

There is great power in God's promises. Even God's law cannot annul them or make them ineffective.[326] Neither can our human frailty and sins prevent their fulfillment. They transform us as we believe, trust and rest in them. The Apostle Peter wrote:

> "His divine power has given to us … *exceedingly great* and *precious promises*, that through these you may be partakers of the *divine nature.*" (2Pt 1:3-4)

Imagine! God's *exceedingly great* and *precious* promises impart His divine nature. Often those who have embraced God's hope-for-all promises have told me how they love others now more than ever before. Since God's love for every person never ends, we are drawn to admire and model Him in His love.[327] What a confirmation of the truth of our hope!

See Peter Hiett's inspiring 21 minute movie highlighting this truth.[328]

The Christ-Honoring Paradigm

Mercy Aiken challenges us with this observation:

> "Traditional doctrines teach us to interpret the victorious scriptures in the light of the judgment scriptures. But what if God wants us to see it the other way around? Is not Christ's victory the greatest revelation in the Bible? Standing on this highest peak—that is, the finished work of the cross, causes us to see a much larger and far more beautiful panoramic view of God's plan throughout the ages. We do not throw out one set of Scriptures in favor of another. Rather, we seek to harmonize them … It is time to stop ignoring the parts of the Bible that do not fit in with our theology."[329]

God's "all" promises are for all people—
*and they **will** be fulfilled.*

ANCHOR 10

Hope in Prophecy

As we saw in Anchor 1, God has a wonderful plan for *all* people, and it originated *before* time began. It can be seen in prophetic utterances throughout the Scriptures. Here are a few examples:

All Prophets Testify

> "Heaven must receive [Christ] *until the times of restoration* [*apokatastasis* G605] of *all* things [especially all people[330]] which God has spoken by the mouth of *all His holy prophets* since the world began." (Acts 3:21)

There is a prophetic timeline to God's plan—*until the times*. It points to a pivotal event in human history, one spoken of by *all* the prophets. Its focus is clearly all persons, as Peter reaffirms:

> "*All* the prophets ... have also *foretold* these days. ... God ... saying to Abraham, 'In your seed *all* the families of the earth shall be blessed.'" (Acts 3:24-25)

God's blessing comes to *all* families, and *all* the prophets have foretold it.

An 890-page, scholarly, historical study details the implications of this restoration—*apokatastasis*—as understood during the first eight centuries of church history.[331]

Further confirming God's prophetic timeline, Peter continued:

> "To you *first* [not exclusively] God, having raised up His Servant Jesus, sent Him to bless you, in turning away *every one of you* from your iniquities." (Acts 3:26)

Note the phrases: "To you *first* ... and *every one* of you." First century Jews were not the only ones to be blessed, merely the first ones. God has an order in fulfilling all His promises—one that spans the ages. *Fourteen* times, Jesus said, "He who has ears to hear, let him hear."[332] Not everyone hears at the same time nor in this age; God decides when that happens.

Prophecies: Israel, Egypt, Sodom

Israel, Egypt and Sodom all underwent severe judgments from God for their rebellion and evil ways. You would think those judgments might have barred all hope of restoration; yet we are told in Scripture that all three, even Sodom, will be restored. I believe these three nations represent all peoples and cultures on the earth, believers and unbelievers alike. More.[333]

Message of Joy Unveiled

Hear these amazing words of Jesus spoken to two distraught disciples just after He died and rose again:

> "O foolish ones and slow of heart to believe in *all* that the prophets have spoken. ... And beginning at Moses and all the Prophets, He expounded to them in all the Scriptures the things concerning Himself. ... *Then* their eyes were *opened* and they knew Him. ... And they said to one another, 'Did not our *heart burn* within us ['were not our *hearts filled with joy*—NLV] ... while He *opened the Scriptures* to us?'"[334]

Are we also foolish ones, slow of heart to believe *all* that the prophets have spoken?

Here is a clue from this passage:

When Jesus opens the Scriptures to us, our hearts should *burn* with *joy*. So if we are *not* experiencing deep joy in our faith, I doubt we have understood the Gospel—what Peter announced as "good news of peace;" Paul as: "good news of God's grace," "gospel of peace ... glad tidings of good things;" the angel as: "good tidings of *great* joy."[335] Joy is at the heart of the Gospel! More examples.[336]

The Jubilee

The Jubilee was an ancient and wondrously prophetic law. Observe what the Lord said to the children of Israel:

> "And you shall consecrate the 50th year and *proclaim liberty throughout all the land* to *all* its inhabitants. It shall be a Jubilee for you; and *each of you* shall return to his possession, and *each of you* shall return to his family." (Lv 25:10)

Once every fifty years, Israel's servants were given their liberty, ancestral lands were restored to their original owners and all debts were cancelled.

Many believe the Jubilee points to the coming of the Messiah as Jesus will release all people from bondage and slavery to sin and death. For example, author and theologian George Sarris writes:

> "A custom in ancient Israel actually foreshadowed an ultimate restoration of all things. ... It didn't prefigure what would happen at the end of an 'age' such as seven years, but what would happen at the end of an 'age of ages'—after 'seven Sabbaths of years'—or 'seven sevens.' ... The great Jubilee Festival foreshadowed what God would ultimately do." More.[337]

The Jubilee is the antithesis of our tradition's doctrine of endless punishment. It is prophetic of the future restoration of all when God becomes "all in all" after all creation is made subject to God in Christ.[338]

All Creation Freed

Paul is likely alluding to the Jubilee's prophetic fulfillment in this awesome declaration:

> "The creation eagerly waits for the revealing of the sons of God. [It] was subjected to futility ... in *hope*; because the *creation* itself also will be delivered from the bondage of corruption into the glorious liberty of the children of God. For we know that the whole creation [which includes humanity] groans and labors

with birth pangs ["suffers the pains of childbirth" NAS] together until now. Not only that, but we also who have the *firstfruits* of the Spirit." (Rom 8:19-23)

All creation will be delivered from corruption (i.e., sin and death) into the glorious liberty of God's *firstfruit* servants.[339] God deserves and receives the whole harvest, not only its initial fruits. David's prophecy affirms it:

"All the ends of the world shall remember and turn to the Lord, and all the families of the nations shall worship before You ... all those who go down to the dust shall bow down before Him,[340] even he who cannot keep himself alive." (Ps 22:27-29)

Christ Comforts All

In Isaiah, the prophet declares:

"The Spirit of the Lord ... has anointed Me to preach the gospel [good news] to the poor; He has sent Me to heal the brokenhearted, to proclaim liberty to the captives and recovery of sight to the blind, to set at liberty those who are oppressed. ... [He closed in saying:] Today this Scripture is fulfilled in your hearing." (Lk 4:18)

These amazing words were prophesied 750 years before Christ.[341] And what makes them *especially* noteworthy is that it was Jesus' first public address—launching, if you will, His public ministry. Naturally then, we would expect something absolutely prophetic and momentous. And it certainly was.

This promised blessing was destined for *every* human being, since Jesus included the following clause in the original account:

"... to comfort *all* who mourn." (Is 61:1-2)

Jesus later confirmed these words in His beatitudes where He said that the poor, hungry and sorrowful people of the world would be blessed.[342]

The Gospel is truly good news of great joy for *all* people. Jesus' message heals the brokenhearted, sets captives free, opens blind eyes, frees the oppressed and comforts *all* who mourn, i.e., everyone![343]

Hope in the Book of Revelation

It is tragic that the book of Revelation, though full of hope, has been misinterpreted as teaching something so horrendous (eternal suffering in a literal lake of fire), that it has driven some people insane.[344]

In Anchor 2, we saw the critical role of symbolism in the Bible—particularly that of fire. This has especially veiled the scope and majesty of the book of Revelation.

Dr. A. Nyland writes, "Due to its symbolic nature, Revelation has been the source of much controversy."[345]

William Barclay admits, "It is the most difficult book in the Bible."[346]

Most would agree that we must not interpret the symbolic writings in a way that contradicts the Bible's clear, non-symbolic truths.

Also, we must realize that Revelation, the last book of the Bible, was written over 4,000 years after Adam and 40 years *after* the Gospels.[347] Surely, God would *not* have withheld vital moral facts about judgment for thousands of years, only to tuck it away at the end of perhaps the most symbolic and difficult-to-understand book of the Bible.

Having considered the nature of this book, let us turn our attention to two of its amazing statements:

> "*Every* creature ... in heaven and on the earth and *under the earth* ... [worshipped God]." (Rv 5:13)

Under the earth is a metaphorical phrase for the abode of the dead, i.e., Hades.[348]

> "Great and wonderful are thy works, O Lord God, the Almighty! Just and true are thy ways, thou king of the nations![349] Who shall not reverence thee, O Lord, and glorify thy name? For thou

alone art holy; therefore all nations shall come and worship before thee, for thy *just judgments have been made plain!*" (Rv 15:3-4 PME)

That's the key element of this book! Once the nations understand the truth about God's *just* judgments, they will come and worship our awesome Father and Creator! Let us meditate on this prophecy until its wonder transforms our hearts. A time *is* coming soon when this promise will be fulfilled!

New Jerusalem

One of the greatest prophecies in the Bible is about Jerusalem.

> "*At that time* [New] Jerusalem shall be called 'The Throne of the Lord' and *all the nations* shall be gathered to it. No more shall they [all the nations] follow the dictates of their evil hearts." (Jer 3:17)[350]

With this amazing Old Testament prophecy as our backdrop, let us now look at ten key points found in the closing chapters of Revelation, which give us great hope for all people:

1) A city from God (New Jerusalem) will come down from heaven and *God will dwell with us.* (Rv 21:2)

This city has a connection to the place of judgment called the "lake of fire." (Rv 21:2, 8-10)

2) God is *actively present* in this city. (Rv 21:3)

3) Just outside the city is a world of lost and sinful people. (Rv 22:14-15)

4) Though sinners are outside the city, its *gates remain open!* (Rv 21:25)

This affirms great hope for those outside.

5) A notorious class of sinners, called "Kings of the earth,"[351] who with the beast and the false prophet stood against the Lord, are *now* saved:

> "The nations will walk by its light, and the *kings of the earth* will bring their glory into it." (Rv 21:24 NAS)[352]

They bring their glory and honor into the city! (Rv 19:19; 21:24)[353]

6) To enter the city, they must first *wash* their robes. (Rv 22:14 NAS)[354]

Professor Thomas Talbott writes:

> "I say 'wash their robes [while] in the lake of fire,' [through the blood of Jesus][355] because where else could those outside the city wash their robes except in the lake of fire? Clearly then, something like that must happen in the lake of fire to enable the kings of the earth and others to enter the city from the only possible position outside its gates, and that something is surely repentance and a thorough cleansing of a kind that implies a proper relationship with Jesus Christ."[356]

7) Priests are *serving* and *reigning* with Christ. (Rv 20:4-6)[357]

Such servants, filled with love for God and neighbor, would be compelled to bring the Good News to those outside—to a world of hurting people.

8) A "tree of life" is in this city with leaves for the "healing" of the nations (peoples). (Rv 22:2)

These "healing" leaves must be for all of the sinful, suffering people outside the city—who else is there? What hope this brings for all people!

9) God's servants *serve* Him and *reign—to the ages of the ages.*[358] (Rv 22:3-5 MYLT)

This means they persist in their efforts *until* they accomplish their goal[359]—to lead every lost person to faith and submission to Jesus Christ, the Lord of all.[360] As helpless sinners trust in Christ, they are forgiven—their robes are washed.[361] They can now enter the Holy City.[362]

Paul said:

> "God ... made us sit together in the heavenly places in Christ Jesus that in the *ages to come* He might *show* [exhibit; display[363]] the *exceeding* riches of His grace." (Eph 2: 4-7)

To whom will God "display" His grace in future ages? To those in greatest need of it—those outside the city.

10) *All* who are thirsty are invited to *freely* take the water of life! (Rv 22:16-17)

These final words of hope are declared in the immediate context of sinners outside the city (v. 15). Who are more thirsty than they? Who longs for their return more than their heavenly Father? He patiently waits, as Jesus so beautifully depicted in the parable of the wayward son.[364]

Vision of Hope and Joy

The closing chapters of the Bible abound with hope for all people, even in the context of the lake of fire.

Let's recap:

A metaphorical "lake of fire" exists in the context of the City of God—a place of divine purification in the very presence of the Lamb.[365] God Himself, a consuming fire,[366] is ever present:

> "If I make my bed in hell [*Sheol*] ... you [God] are there."
> (Ps 139:8)

The gates of the city never close, yet there is a multitude of sinners outside, who to some degree, are experiencing God's loving, purifying fire. Sinners are "saved" and then enter the city. There are servants of God and priests reigning, implying ministry to those still outside the gates. There are nations of suffering people who need the healing leaves of the tree of life. An invitation to all is given!

> "The Spirit and the bride [Christ's followers[367]] say, 'Come!' And let him who hears say, 'Come!' And let him who thirsts come. Whoever desires, let him take the water of life freely." (Rv 22:16-17)

Everyone is invited! Nothing bars sinners (all of us) from receiving God's mercy and reconciliation, since "the long-suffering of the Lord *is* salvation."[368] And when does His long-suffering end? Never.

Furthermore, it's the Spirit of Christ *with His bride* who are inviting them. This is very significant and confirms everything said above. Praise God! Jesus, whose name means *Savior*, will fulfill His mission to save the world.[369]

Sinners "outside" will at some point, bow their knees and worship Jesus Christ as Lord.[370] They will repent—wash their robes in Christ's blood and follow Him in keeping His commands. They will be given new names[371] and the right to the tree of life, as so many others have. We know this is true, since God doesn't change.[372] This gives us great peace and security.

> "I saw a new heaven and a new earth. ... God ... will wipe away *every* tear from their eyes." (Rv 21:1, 4a)

> "There shall be *no more* death, *nor* sorrow, *nor* crying ... *no more* pain." (Rv 21:4b)

> "Behold, I make *all* things [or all humanity—TNT[373]] new." (Rv 21:5)

What great hope is found in these closing chapters of the Bible!

God's Love Prevails! Not *Hades*.

Jesus told Peter:

> "I will build my church, and the gates of hell [*Hades*] shall not prevail against it [or *prevail in resisting it*—TNT note]." (Mt 16:18 KJV) More examples.[374]

"Gates" in ancient times were part of the wall protecting cities from its enemies; they served a *defensive* purpose—to keep enemies out. So *Hades'* metaphorically *closed* gates, adjacent to the Holy City's *open* gates, are powerless to keep Jesus or His servants out as indicated in the verses above. In fact, Jesus already stormed its gates[375] and, with His church, will continue doing so. Remember, He holds its keys[376] along with His servant priests who will reign with Him.[377]

Jesus specifically came to set the captives free[378] and to lead captivity *itself* captive![379] Surely this includes the captivity of *Hades, Gehenna* and the metaphorical lake of fire.

God—All in All

It was not the apostle John in Revelation who spoke of the very end. That honor was given to the apostle Paul.[380] Please note carefully what I have italicized in 1Cor 15:22-25, 28:

> "*Just as all* men die in Adam, *so all* men will be brought to life in Christ [JB]. *But* each one *in his own order*:
>
> Christ the *first-fruits* [1st order],
>
> *afterward* those who are Christ's at His coming [2nd order].
>
> *Then* comes the *end, when* He delivers the kingdom to God the Father, *when* He puts an end to all rule ... authority and power. For He must reign *till* He has put all enemies under His feet. ...
>
> *Now when* all [people[381] are subjected[382]] to Him [3rd order—all people have now repented—submitted themselves to Christ] ...

then the Son Himself [as Son of Man] will also be subject to Him [as humanity's representative head]

that God may be *all* in *all* [everything to everyone[383]]."

The subjection to Christ that we see in this passage is *not* one of compulsion. Both the submission of Jesus to the Father and that of His enemies to Him stem from the *same* Greek word in the *same* verse.[384] This is a willing submission from the heart by all parties. God cannot nor will not be "all" in that which is false. Furthermore, Paul used this same word in the context of the righteousness of faith.[385]

Note these "time" words: "in his own order," "first-fruits," "afterward," "then," "end," "when," "till," "now when," and "then." These terms and phrases reveal a timeline involving three categories of individuals: Christ; His followers; All humanity. This has not happened yet. All enemies have not *yet* submitted themselves to Christ ... but they will—God has purposed it.[386] And when it occurs, Christ will again submit Himself to God afresh as our representative head—the "Son of Man." *Then* God will become *all* in *all people* [387] filling us with Himself, the crowning glory of our salvation. Jesus truly fulfills His role and His title as the "Savior of the world."[388]

When God is truly known in all His splendor, limitless grace and love—even in judgment, *all* people will worship Him.[389]

All Will Worship God

- "*All* the families of the nations shall worship." (Ps 22:27b)
- "*All* the earth shall worship You and sing praises." (Ps 66:4)
- "*All* kings shall fall down before Him." (Ps 72:11a)
- "*All* nations shall ... worship and glorify Him." (Ps 86:9)
- "*All* the kings of the earth shall praise You." (Ps 138:4)
- "*All* Your works shall praise You." (Ps 145:10)
- "*All* nations and peoples of every language worshipped him." (Dn 7:14 NIV)
- "*All* nations shall come and worship before You, for Your judgments have been manifested." (Rv 15:4b)

Two thousand years ago Jesus said these words:

> "I still have many things to say to you, but you cannot bear (or handle[390]) them now. However, when He, the Spirit of truth has come, He will guide you into all truth." More.[391]

Fifteen hundred years after Jesus said those words, a Catholic priest in Germany saw amazing things in his Bible that captured his heart. Through the newly invented printing press of that time, Martin Luther was enabled to bypass the religious gatekeepers of his day [392] and get his message to his entire nation. His discovery changed the world.[393]

Was the Spirit of truth guiding Luther's heart? If so, why did God wait 1500 years to reveal these things to someone? As Jesus said, we couldn't handle it then—perhaps even for centuries to follow. One thousand years is only a day to God.[394] And note! Not everything was revealed to Luther.[395] The greatest revelation of all is the limitless scope of God's love and power—God *ultimately* becoming *all* in *all*.

My heart rejoices over the words of *another* Catholic priest,[396] spoken 500 years after Luther—only half a day in God's eyes:

> "The Lord has redeemed all of us, all of us, with the Blood of Christ: all of us. ... Everyone! ... Even the atheists. Everyone!"—Pope Francis, spiritual leader of 1.2 billion Catholics.[397]

Might this heart-warming quote, by the Pope himself in 2013 AD, be prophetic coming at this time in human history? I can't say for sure. But the prophet Isaiah said: "In the last days ... the LORD's temple will be established ... and all nations [peoples] will stream to it."[398]

Is our Heavenly Father revealing the wonders of His being like never before?[399] I believe He is. And today's technology far exceeds Luther's printing press in bringing Good News of Great Joy for All People!

All God's holy prophets spoke of these things
since the world began. Now it's our turn!

Ten Anchors Summarized

1. Hope in History: *God's promises and actions in Biblical history demonstrate His prevailing love for all people.*

2. Hope in Fire: *God's loving and consuming fires transform us into His image.*

3. Hope in Judgment: *God's judgments serve a good purpose.*

4. Hope in Ancient Greek: *Ancient Greek does not teach endless punishment.*

5. Hope in Death: *Nothing can separate us from God's love and mercy—not death, not destruction, not Gehenna. ... Nothing!*

6. Hope in Justice: *God's justice assures us that endless punishment is not Biblical—loving correction and mercy are!*

7. Hope in Our Father: *God is everyone's loving Father.*

8. Hope in God's Nature: *God loves every person and always will. He has all the time and power to transform every heart without violating anyone's will. **His** will and love prevail.*

9. Hope in God's Promises: *God's "all" promises are for all people—and they **will** be fulfilled.*

10. Hope in Prophecy: *All God's holy prophets spoke of these things since the world began. Now it's our turn.*

This is Good News of Great Joy for All People!

Bible Interpretation

Translation Differences

When we read the Bible, we are not reading the exact words and thoughts of Jesus and the apostles but rather the interpretation of the ancient writings by English translators.[400]

This is critical, since the background of most translators includes belief in endless punishment. So naturally, they interpret judgment passages from that view. I do not fault them for being human. My point is that this bias makes our study very challenging.[401]

So, what can we do?

We should cross-check judgment warnings with an array of translations relying on the Holy Spirit to open our understanding.

The Holy Spirit

Reading the Bible without the Holy Spirit is like a blind man on a bicycle. Only God can reveal the truth of the Scriptures to our hearts.[402]

If a judgment passage seems unfair or contradicts God's unfailing love and mercy for all people, we should commit it to the Lord *until* He opens our understanding. Let us not cower from questioning what seems wrong. Jesus and Paul exhort us in this.[403]

We are not judged for being incorrect about a matter but for how we live our lives.[404] If radical religious extremists would courageously question the violent teachings of their faith, the world would be far better off. And we, in the West, are *not* immune to that same spirit. Examine history. Even the Apostle Paul proves my point.[405]

Understanding Difficult Passages—Key Points

1) Our Bibles are translations and, as such, require us to look deeper when facing troubling passages.[406]

2) Scripture needs to be understood in context.[407]

3) Scripture interprets Scripture.[408]

4) Recognize and respect the extreme use of Bible symbolism.[409]

5) God's judgments ultimately serve a good purpose.[410]

6) Learn the true meaning of the ancient terms pertaining to human destiny.[411]

7) God's judgments are just and synergistic with His mercy.[412]

8) Justice will not violate our God-given conscience.[413]

9) Our view of God's nature and character determines how we interpret Scripture.[414]

10) Only Christ can open our understanding of Scripture.[415]

11) Though we only know God's judgments in *part,* yet we can rest assured of His prevailing love in them.[416]

12) Christ's victory ought to be the lens through which we interpret all judgment warnings.[417]

Questions Considered

It is assumed that you have read and understood the ten Anchors of Hope in this book. They lay a foundation for my responses—the endnotes add important details. My answers are brief and tentative—since I only know in part.[418] My authority is Scripture and the Holy Spirit as I seek His light.

"It pleased the Father ... to reconcile all things [esp. people] ... **having made peace through the blood of His cross."** [419]

If the Father reconciles all to Himself ...

1) Why did **Jesus die** if God also judges us according to our deeds?
2) Why **preach** the Gospel?
3) Why not **party** and live it up?
4) How do we know **"all"** means "everyone"?
5) How do we know **"all things"** includes people?
6) Only the **"righteous"** inherit God's Kingdom, correct?
7) What about the **"wrath"** of God?
8) Why did John say "that the world '**might**' be saved"?
9) What about "perish" in **John 3:16**?
10) What about "**damnation**"?
11) What about "**resurrection to be condemned**"?
12) What about "**eternal condemnation**"?
13) What about "**everlasting destruction**"?
14) What about the "**terror**" of the Lord?
15) Some say there's **not one verse** that offers hope for salvation after death. Is that true?
16) What does it mean to seek God "**while**" He may be found?
17) What about the destruction of **soul and body**?

18) What about "**losing**" the soul?
19) Can one's name be forever "**blotted out**" of the Book of Life?
20) What about the sin that is **"never"** forgiven?
21) What about the "**narrow gate**," "depart from me" and "weeping and grinding of teeth"?
22) What about the **furnace** of fire?
23) What about **Sodom** and Gomorrah suffering the vengeance of eternal fire?
24) What about the **rich man** in hell?
25) What about the **unquenchable** fire?
26) What about tormented in the **lake of fire?**
27) What about the **smoke** of their torment going up forever?
28) What about the **undying worm?**
29) What about the **burned branches**?
30) Isn't **repentance** impossible if we fall away?
31) What about alleged **visions** from hell?
32) Why would it have been better if **Judas** had not been born?
33) Did God really "hate" **Esau**?
34) What about **Hitler**—how could he ever be forgiven?
35) Doesn't **justice** demand infinite penalty for sin because it is committed against an infinite, holy God?
36) How can we trust our **conscience** if our heart is wicked?
37) Why didn't God make this **plain**?
38) What about all the **suffering** in the world?
39) Isn't this a **false teaching** of the "last days"?
40) Isn't this **wishful thinking**—too good to be true?
41) Is this **Universalism**?
42) What Bible **translations** do you use?

"It pleased the Father ... to reconcile all things [esp. people[420]] **having made peace through the blood of His cross."** [421]

If the Father reconciles all people to Himself ...

1) Why did Jesus die if God also judges us according to our deeds?

Jesus died to reconcile us to our Father as quoted above.[422] But what does reconciliation look like? In one word: Jesus. The purpose of our lives is to become *like* Jesus—what salvation is all about. But how does that happen? It starts by knowing God as our loving Father—a Father determined to see Jesus shining through us. This is why His forgiveness *and* His judgments work hand-in-hand. You see, there are *two* dimensions in forgiveness: *redemptive:* based on Jesus' sacrifice[423] and *relational:* based on our responses to God's Spirit working in our hearts.[424] Understanding this distinction helps us appreciate why our Father rightly holds us accountable for our actions. His mercy *and* judgments work together for our good. This resolves many questions.[425]

2) Why preach the Gospel?

The love of Christ compels us[426] as people all around us are hurting *right now.* Everyone longs for peace and hope especially in their fear of death.[427] When Jesus saw the crowds, He was moved with compassion because they were distressed and dispirited.[428] We have truly Good News a hurting world longs to hear: "How beautiful are the feet of those who preach the gospel of peace, who bring *glad tidings* of *good things!*"[429] Also, our Lord commands us[430] and it's a great privilege and pleasure to do so.[431] Simply put, the Gospel brings peace for troubled minds, purpose in life and transforms our character.[432]

3) Why not party and live it up if all are reconciled?

This question reveals a misapprehension of what reconciliation implies.[433] Salvation is ultimately becoming like Christ—His values and priorities becoming ours. We no longer live for ourselves but for Him who gave His all for us. In addition, there are consequences to how we live as discussed in Anchor 6, "Justice and God's Law."[434]

HOPE FOR ALL   133

4) How do we know "all" means "everyone" in God's reconciliation-of-all promises?

"All" means everyone unless the context implies otherwise. Dr. Keith DeRose[435] says: "When the domain is limited, there has to be some fairly clear clue about what the limited domain is. ... The Biblical writers aren't so incompetent as to mean some specially restricted class that doesn't clearly present itself."[436] If we read God's "all" promises in context *and* in light of these ten Anchors of Hope, we are assured they refer to everyone.

5) How do we know "all things" include people in God's "all" promises such as Col 1:19-20?

In this passage for example, verse 21 clearly specifies that people are in view: "and *you* [a person], who once were alienated and enemies in your mind by wicked works, yet now He has reconciled." It's not frogs, fish and flowers that need reconciliation; it's people! In addition, this reconciliation brings *peace through the blood of His cross.* Christ died for *four* specific classifications of persons,[437] not for inanimate objects. More.[438]

6) Only the "righteous" inherit God's Kingdom, correct? 1Cor 6:9

Yes, the "unrighteous," *while* in that condition, cannot inherit it. But we will not always be unrighteous. We all come to Christ in an "unrighteous" state,[439] but then God works righteousness into us.[440] Throughout the ages, God will continue transforming us until we all fully reflect the image of Christ.[441]

7) What about the "wrath" of God? Rom 1:18; Jn 3:36

The word "anger,"[442] not wrath, is used in many translations.[443] The NEB reads: "retribution" which harmonizes with "measured" judgment as Jesus taught.[444] Anger is defined as "extreme or passionate displeasure."[445] God's wrath then, would be His passionate displeasure and just recompense of sinful conduct, dealt with fairly according to deeds[446] and seasoned with mercy[447] as He determines best for each person.

God's "anger" should be seen as something positive and purposeful. More.[448]

8) Why did John say God sent His Son that the world "might" be saved? Jn 3:17 KJV

This wording has been gravely misunderstood. God does not hope to save but does save. Many translations say clearly that God sent Jesus *to save* the world.[449] Nonetheless, "might" in the KJV can certainly mean "will." For example: "All this was done, that the scripture … *might* be fulfilled."[450] "He ordained twelve … that He *might* send them forth to preach."[451] He made us sit in the heavens "that in the ages to come He *might* shew the exceeding riches of His grace."[452] Is there any doubt that these "mights" mean "will"? More.[453]

9) What about "perish" in John 3:16-17?

"For God so loved the world that He gave His one and only Son, that whoever believes [trusts, abides] in Him shall not perish [*be perishing*—CLT; or remain lost[454]] but have eternal life [i.e., *life of the Age*[455]—which Jesus defined as knowing God[456]]. **For** God did *not* send His Son into the world to condemn the world, but **to save** *the world*[457] through Him."[458]

It's true that *while* in "unbelief" (resisting the things of God) we cannot experience true life—*characteristic of the life of God in the age to come.*[459] But unbelief is *not* a hopeless state or no one could *ever* believe.

"Perish" and "lost" are translated from the same Greek word—*apollumi* G622. To be "lost" then is the prerequisite to being saved or made whole![460] Jesus came to save the "lost"—the perishing.[461] He came to save sinners—specifically to save us *from* our sins—"turning *every one of us from* our wicked ways."[462] For more on salvation.[463]

Jesus put it this way: "And this is eternal life [life in the Age[464]], that they may know You, the only true God, and Jesus Christ whom You have sent." And God said: "*All* shall *know* Me, from the least ... to the greatest. ... For I *will be merciful.*"[465]

The key is this: God has *not* limited salvation to this short life. *All* the "dead" (which includes the lost—the perishing) live to Him. "For He is not the God of the dead but of the living, for *all live* to Him."[466]

10) What about "damnation"? Mt 23:33 KJV

The English word "damnation," inferring endless punishment, is based on the common Greek word for judgment—*krisis* G2920. It should *never* have been translated "damnation." Most Bible translations do not use this word.[467] "Damnation" is found 11 times in the King James Version but *not once* in the New King James Version.

11) What about "resurrection to be condemned"? Jn 5:29 NIV

Again, the Greek behind the word "condemned" is *krisis* G2920, the common word for judgment. The NAS, along with most translations, say "resurrection of (to) judgment." Tragically, the word "condemned" is erroneously associated with damnation as a result of the KJV's long-standing tradition. Furthermore, the word "condemned" does not specify duration. Judges in our courts condemn those found guilty to corrective institutions, but only until their sentences are complete.

12) What about "eternal condemnation"? Gal 1:8-9 NIV

Neither the word "eternal" nor the word "condemn" is used in the original Greek. The word is *anathĕma.*[468] The CEV translates Gal 1:9: *"God will punish."* The NCV and EXB translate it: *"judged guilty."* Most translations say *accursed*—defined as "a solemn invocation of supernatural wrath."[469] Note that Paul wished *anathĕma* on himself, and some Jews bound themselves to *anathĕma* if they did not fast until they killed Paul.[470] Neither Paul nor the Jews wished endless pain on themselves. For the Jews, it meant starvation; for Paul, it was righteous judgment.[471]

13) What about "everlasting destruction"? 2Thes 1:8-9

MYLT: "who shall suffer *justice—age-during* destruction."[472] Prof. D. B. Hart, (NTAT): "Exacting justice ... Who will pay the just reparation of ruin in the Age." TNT: "who will proceed paying the thing that is right: ruin pertaining to the Age [of Messiah]."[473] God's justice is always "according to works" and thus measured and limited, i.e., "age-during."[474] Also God does not take "vengeance" as worded in many translations—the Greek is "justice."[475]

14) What about the "terror" of the Lord? 2Cor 5:11

"Terror" is based on the same Greek word normally translated fear (*phobos* G5401) from which we get our English "phobia." Most translations read "fear." SNT and CEV say "respect." Dr. A. Nyland writes, "The Greeks used it [*phobos*] in the meaning of "respect" when used in the case of gods or things sacred."[476] Compare translations! God is not a terrorist.

15) Some say there's not one verse that offers hope for salvation after death. Is that true?

Absolutely not.[477] This book shows otherwise. Here's one: "The gospel was preached *even to those who are dead*."[478] Tragically many translations add "now" before "dead"—which means: it was preached to people *while* they were living but who *have since* died. This changes its meaning entirely. Of course the Bible offers no hope in death if its supporting texts are altered.[479]

16) What does it mean to seek God "while" He may be found? Is 55:6-7

In context, this relates to Israel (of which Paul says all will be saved—Rom 11:26) and had a national application.[480] Yet there's a sense of urgency for us all. Our Father has great patience with His children, but if we persistently resist Him, He will discipline us as necessary. In the meantime, He may step back out of view for a time *until* some necessary lessons are learned.[481] But note what follows next! "Let the wicked forsake his way. ... Let him return to the Lord, and He *will have mercy* on him; and ... *will abundantly pardon.*" God's promises of mercy are clear. We can rest assured and rejoice in them.[482]

17) What about the destruction of both soul and body in *Gehenna*? Mt. 10:28-31; Lk 12:4-7

Jesus says to His disciples (MSG), "Don't be bluffed into silence by the threats of bullies. There's nothing they can do to your soul, your core being. Save your fear for God, who holds your entire life—body and soul—in his hands."[483]

Then Jesus *immediately* reassures them of their Heavenly Father's loving care—that He even numbers the hairs on their heads ... And *then* He concludes ... *"So don't be afraid."*[484]

What? Don't be afraid? How could He say that if He had just threatened them with endless torment? They would have been terrified! Any soothing words, at this point, would be useless. The reason He could calm their fears was because endless pain was not at all on their minds. More.[485]

18) What about "losing" the soul? Mt 16:26-27

The Jerusalem Bible reads: "What then will a man gain if he wins the whole world and *ruins* his *life?*" Note carefully what follows: "He will *reward* [*repay* RSV[486]] each one *according to* his behavior." To ruin one's life is directly linked to being repaid "according to his behavior." This implies a specific, limited judgment[487] resulting in some kind of serious loss.[488]

Jesus said, "If you want to be *perfect* go [the whole way—NEB] sell what you have and give to the poor, and you will have *treasure* in heaven."[489] Rewards or loss are at stake, not endless punishment.[490]

19) Can one's name be forever "blotted out" of the Book of Life? Rv 3:5

It seems the "Book of Life" is one of many metaphors for Jesus such as: "Author of Life," "Bread of Life," "Resurrection and Life," "Word of Life.," etc.[491] It brings me great comfort knowing that the Book of Life is our precious Savior.

If we are not abiding in Christ, we are living a deprived life—"blotted out" of His abundant life—deprived of the great joy that comes with loving others. We could also be deprived from the great honor of ruling with Christ in His future millennial Kingdom.[492]

Yet remember: God's love prevails. He *never* gives up on us. Though Israel was "cut-off" (blotted out) they will be grafted in again.[493] And what He does for Israel, He does for all.[494]

20) What about the sin that is "never" forgiven?
Mk 3:28-30 (cp Mt 12:31-32)

Prof. D. B. Hart (NTAT) renders it: "But whoever blasphemes against the Spirit, the Holy one, has no excuse throughout the age [neither in this age nor in the one that is coming—Mt 12:32] but is answerable for a transgression in the Age. Because they said, 'He has an *impure spirit.*'"[495]

This translation, along with others,[496] does not say this sin shall "never" be forgiven. The "sin" committed is *thinking* that Jesus has an impure spirit[497]—which in effect, destroys (in one's mind) His credibility *to* forgive. So long as such blindness exists—during this age and into the next, His forgiveness cannot be sought. But a time will come when all blindness will be removed and forgiveness will be sought and received.[498] Furthermore, the text does *not* say there's no forgiveness in a subsequent age for Paul spoke of the "ages" (plural) to come in which God *reveals* "the *exceeding* [*immeasurable*[499]] riches of His grace in His kindness towards us."[500]

With God's *immeasurable* grace revealed in ages to come, and God's "all" promises presented in Anchors 1 and 10, we are more than justified to believe that God's love will ultimately prevail for all humanity. And even *if* the judgment of this sin were not forgiven (as unlikely as that is), it does *not* alter the fact that our Father's "lawful" penalties are always just and in character with His loving heart for all.[501]

21) What of the "narrow gate," "depart from me" and "weeping and grinding of teeth [sorrow and regret— TNT]? Lk 13:23-35 (cp Mt 8:12; 13:42, 50; 22:13; 24:51; 25:30)

In context, the *sorrow* and *regret* refer to the Jewish leadership of first-century Judea (in Jerusalem) losing its place of leadership in God's reign. This doesn't ignore a personal application. All three phrases in this question are found in Luke 13:22-35 of which verse 30 may be the key that unlocks the meaning of these parables.

"'Lord, are there few who are [*being*[502]] saved?' *Strive* to enter through the narrow gate,[503] for many ... will seek to enter and will not be able [will not have the strength[504]]. ... *Indeed* there are last who will be first and there are *first who will be last.*"[505]

Observe: those who came first were found lacking—did not qualify for a place of honor in the Kingdom. Others, who came after them, were immediately honored.[506] But later, ... the "first" ones return and are granted the right to enter as the "*first who will be last.*" The word "indeed" assures us of this.

Apparently, those who came first needed more time to mature, suffering the consequences of their choices. Though sorrow and regret[507] are part of the maturing process, joy is its end. "His anger is but a moment. ... Weeping may endure for a night, but joy comes in the morning."[508] This is exactly what follows!

"O Jerusalem, Jerusalem ... How often I wanted to gather your children together, as a hen gathers her brood under her wings, but you were not willing! See! Your house is left to you *desolate*; and *assuredly*, I say to you, you shall not see Me *until* the time comes when you say, '*Blessed is He who comes in the name of the Lord!*'"[509]

This passage is *not* about endless penalty.[510] The "first" who suffered desolation, finally recognize and honor the *Savior of the World!*[511] All Israel shall be saved![512]

22) What about the furnace of fire? Mt 13:42, 50

Israel's fiery furnace also sheds light on the above parables:

"I will ... *remove your filthiness completely*. ... You shall defile yourself. ... *Then* you shall know that I am the Lord. ... The house of Israel has become dross [useless[513]] to Me. ... I will ... blow on you with the fire of My wrath. ... As silver is melted in the midst of a *furnace,* so shall you be melted in its midst."[514]

Jesus, the promised Messiah sent first to Israel,[515] would certainly use judgment terms in harmony with their sacred Scriptures. We can rest assured about the purifying nature of this fiery furnace.

23) What about Sodom and Gomorrah suffering the vengeance of eternal fire? Jude 1:7 KJV

The PME reads, "Sodom and Gomorrah ... stand in their punishment as a permanent warning of the fire of judgment." The fire no longer burns, but its warning continues!

The CLT: "Sodom ... experiencing the *justice* of fire *eonian*."[516] The MYLT: "Sodom ... an *example*, of fire *age-during, justice* suffering." "Justice" assures us this judgment is limited.[517]

Regarding "vengeance," Prof. Marvin Vincent states that the "RSV [and most others] rightly substitute punishment for vengeance, since *dikē* G1349 carries the underlying idea of right or justice,[518] not necessarily implied in the word 'vengeance.'"[519]

God will raise up, judge (discipline; correct) and restore each citizen of Sodom.[520]

24) What about the rich man in hell (G *Hades*) separated from heaven by an impassible chasm? Lk 16:19-31

A chasm separates the rich man in *Hades* and Abraham. It merely implies that while this judgment endures one cannot cross the chasm. It does not say it is permanent. The chasm is a barrier like *Gehenna's* prison bars of Matthew 5 which imprisons *until* the last cent is paid.[521] Luke 16 does not contradict Matthew 5. No chasm is eternal: "Every valley [chasm] shall be filled and every mountain ... brought low. ... All flesh shall see the salvation of God."[522] No created thing (including chasms) can separate us from God's love.[523] A time is coming when *Hades* itself will release its captives![524]

25) What about the unquenchable fire? Mk 9:43-44

We as human beings cannot extinguish this fire because it is God's fire, hence the word "unquenchable." It is relentless *until* it achieves its purpose.[525] MYLT says the fire is "not being" quenched—present tense. See also CLT, TNT.[526] Some translators have erroneously added "never" to the single Greek word *asbestos*, defined as "not extinguished."[527] The NAS, with many other translations, accurately reads "the unquenchable fire" without the word "never."[528] Furthermore, the context confirms this as a purifying fire—something good.[529]

26) What about *tormented* in the lake of fire? Rv 20:12-15; 21:8

Rev. Charles H. Pridgeon[530] wrote: "To any Greek, or any trained in the Greek language, a 'lake of fire and brimstone' would mean a 'lake of divine purification.'"[531]

The word "torment" associated with this judgment does not mean torture. The word is *basanizo* G928. "Torture" is a different word used once in the NT—committed by humans *not* God.[532] *Basanizo* also describes a ship "tossed" by the waves,[533] "toiling" in rowing a boat[534] and "troubled" by the misconduct of others.[535] These concepts are *not* torture.[536]

Brimstone, in *fire and brimstone,* is the element sulfur[537] used by pagan priests 2,000 years before Christ. Pre-Roman civilizations used it as a medicine, fumigant and bleaching agent. Pliny reported it had medicinal virtues. Romans used it as insecticide to purify a sick room and cleanse its air of evil. The same uses were reported by Homer in 1000 B.C.[538]

The TNT reads: "And he will be *examined*[539] (scrutinized with the touchstone to test his 'mettle') within Fire and Deity (divine qualities) ... in the presence of (before) ... the little Lamb."[540] It comforts me that this purification occurs in Jesus' presence.[541] And John, the writer of Revelation, clearly stated the limited nature of this metaphorical fire.[542]

27) What about the smoke of their torment going up forever and ever [lit. *to ages of ages*—MYLT]? [543] Rv 14:10-11

Compare this with Babylon's judgment a few chapters later in the same book: "Her smoke rises up forever and ever [lit. *to the ages of the ages*—MYLT]."[544] Yet Babylon's judgment was executed in one hour[545]—and its smoke has long since ceased. This gives us further reason to believe that the lake of fire judgment is also not endless.[546] Though the pains and smoke of Babylons fires are past, its judgment warning continues.

28) What about the undying worm? Mk 9:44-49; Is 66:24

This refers to a graphic scene of earthly judgment in Isaiah.[547] Chan and Sprinkle, in *Erasing Hell*, admit there's nothing here that says the souls of the dead are still being tormented.[548] It means the shame of defeat.[549] A few verses earlier (Is 66:6), Isaiah says the Lord "fully" repays His enemies. Endless punishment can never "fully" repay; only a measured judgment can.[550]

In Mark 9, the word "for" links "hell [*Gehenna*] fire," "worm" and "unquenched fire" with the fire that purifies everyone.[551] "For" (*gár* G1063) expresses the reason for what came before,[552] yet *half* of the translations I checked left it out! Not only does this passage *not* teach eternal punishment, it affirms that *Gehenna fire* purifies.

29) What about the burned branches? Jn 15:1-2, 6

Verse 6 of the PME reads: "The man who does not share my life is like a branch that is broken off and withers away. He becomes just like the dry sticks that men pick up and use for the firewood." When we are in vital union with Christ—infused with His love and compassion for others—we become a shining light, a light that in some mysterious way draws people to God.[553] Whereas, if we live selfishly, we are lost in the shadows ... and our loving Father is compelled to bring us through His refining fire. More.[554]

30) Isn't repentance impossible if we fall away?

There's a text which says that if someone falls away, it is impossible to bring them back to repentance.[555] My questions are: *For whom* is it impossible, for God or humans—pastors, counselors, or friends in faith? *When* is it impossible—while on earth or in the age to come? And why is such a person "near" being cursed and not actually cursed?[556] The text does not answer these vital questions. Our only recourse is to keep our faith anchored on the truths that *are* clear--*Nothing* is impossible for God![557]—He who can raise children from lifeless stones[558]—give *new* hearts to the unrepentant![559] We must interpret this in light of God's justice,[560] His Father-heart, His nature of limitless love and power, His "all" promises and His prophetic utterances.[561]

31) What about alleged visions from hell?

If an endless hell were a danger to every person on earth, a loving and just God would have revealed it to everyone.[562] But most of all, my source of truth is the Bible and God's Spirit as He reveals it, not the dreams and illusions of others—whoever they are.[563] We are called to preach *glad tidings of good things—good news of great joy—good news of peace;* not horrific news of great and eternal terror.[564] No one is called to that. Jesus said, "Peace I leave you, My peace I give to you ... *Let not your heart be troubled, neither let it be afraid*.[565] Bring every thought into captivity to the obedience of Christ.[566] These visions only lead us into sin.[567]

32) Why would it have been better if Judas had not been born?
Mt 26:24b

The CLT reads, "The Son of Mankind is indeed going away ... yet woe to that man through whom the Son of Mankind is being given up! Ideal were it for Him if that man were not born!" Could this be right? It's logical for Jesus to have suffered great heart-ache in being betrayed by a close friend.[568] However, even if the common view is right, it does *not* say it would have been better for Judas if his mother had never conceived him, but that he had not been born. Eccl 6:3 says: "If a man begets a hundred children and lives many years ... but ... is not satisfied with goodness. ... I say that a stillborn child is better than he [i.e., it would have been good for Judas if he had not been born—but stillborn]."[569] In any case, nothing here requires us to assume that Judas' destiny is endless pain. See my video.[570]

33) Did God really "hate" Esau? Mal 1:2-3

No. This was hyperbole like Christ's command to "hate" our family, or when Jesus referred to Peter as Satan.[571] Hyperbole was very common in the ancient east.[572] Though Esau "despised" his birthright, he repented[573] and God greatly blessed him.[574] Jesus—then embodiment of God's love for all, died for Esau too.

34) What about Hitler—how could he ever be forgiven?

Jesus died for *all* sinners—including Hitler. No one merits salvation. It all comes down to our faith in the power of God to change any heart and His will to do so.

35) Doesn't justice demand infinite penalty for sin because it is committed against an infinite, holy God?

This is a philosophical idea not based on Scripture. The Bible teaches the opposite. God's holy and true principle of justice originates in "measured" judgment—a tutor bringing us to Christ, *then onto* mercy which triumphs over judgment.[575]

36) How can we trust our conscience if our heart is wicked?
Jer 17:9

Abraham, Jesus and Paul all appeal to it[576] when exhorting us to judge what is right in our search for Truth.[577] Though the KJV says the human heart is wicked,[578] the NAS says it is sick and the Greek OT says it is deep—all regarding the *same verse!* The Greek OT, in this verse, connects examining our "deep" hearts to God's *just* (measured) judgment![579] These descriptions of the human heart are radically different. Sure the human heart is not perfect and can be terribly sick at times, but it can still discern good from evil.[580] See Anchor 6, "The Unwritten Law."

37) Why didn't God make this plain?

Controversy in the Christian faith is extensive and not unique to ultimate destiny.[581] Few realize that endless punishment was *not* the prevailing view of the early church during its first 500 years when the New Testament was read in Greek—not handicapped by translations. The Church inherently knew the true meaning of judgment terms.[582] However, many ancient Fathers thought endless punishment was a necessary deterrent to societal chaos.[583] Jesus told His disciples there were many things He could tell them, but they were not ready.[584] So perhaps the time has come--the Church is ready for the higher revelation of God's limitless grace.[585] The internet age is here and the truth can no longer be suppressed by the institutional gatekeepers of formal religion.

38) What about all the suffering in the world?

I find great comfort in knowing that all the world's suffering and injustices will be made right. The poor, the hungry and the sorrowing (which represent all human suffering) will be eternally blessed.[586] "What we suffer now in this world is nothing compared to the *magnificent future* [PME] God has for us."[587] It comforts me to know that God "is" Love,[588] makes everything beautiful in its time,[589] wipes away all tears and removes all pain.[590]

39) Isn't this a false teaching of the "last days"? Mt 24:11; 2Pt 2:1

No. It's a **true** teaching of the last days! Jeremiah said that the anger [wrath] of the Lord will not turn back *until* He has executed and performed the thoughts and intents of His heart and that in the *latter days* we will understand it perfectly."[591] He repeats it *again*.[592] And Isaiah said, "In the *last days* ... the LORD's temple will be established ... and *all* nations will stream to it."[593] These prophecies affirm that our revelation is of God, since *this is precisely what we believe*. God's wrath is *not* endless but only *until* He has accomplished the loving intents of His heart.[594]

40) Isn't this wishful thinking—too good to be true?

A thing is not false simply because we wish it were true. The truth is, this hope is too good *not* to be true!

41) Is this Universalism?

No—if by that you mean *all roads* lead to heaven. Maybe—if you mean Jesus searches for His lost sheep *until* He finds them no matter what road they're on.[595]

42) What Bible translations do you use?

I've preferred the NKJV mainly for its alternative Greek manuscript footnotes. Also, I'm familiar with it—having memorized many passages over the years. Recently, I've starting reading *The New Testament: A Translation,* by David Bentley Hart.[596] More.[597]

In Closing ...

The most important thing to know is that *only* Christ—the Truth can open the Scriptures to our understanding. It's not just comparing translations. And how do we know He's done so? Joy and peace fill our hearts! "Did not our heart burn within us [were *filled with joy*–NLV] while ... He *opened* the Scriptures to us?"[598]

Jesus Says ...

"Come to Me ... I am gentle and lowly in heart, and you will find rest for your souls. For My yoke is easy and My burden is light." More.[599]

It is my prayer that our Lord and Savior has opened your heart to the wondrous news that our Creator and Father loves every one of us with a love that never fails or ends. Indescribable joy[600] awaits you when Christ anchors this truth in your heart: God's love **will** prevail.

> "May the God of hope fill you with all joy and peace in believing, that you may abound in hope ..." (Rom 15:13)

Author Invitation

Has this book thrilled your heart? If so, would you tell me how? I would love to hear your story. Email or call me.

Read *Hope for All* free online. Invite your friends to read it too! HopeforAllFellowship.com

Share-the-Hope-Books: only $5 HopeforAllFellowship.com/Order

Listen to Hope: audio edition of my first book: *Hope Beyond Hell* HopeforAllFellowship.com/Learn

Learn more about our Hope: HopeforAllFellowship.com/Learn

Connect with others! We're not meant to live isolated lives. Jesus said when two or three of us are together because of Him, you can be sure He'll be there. (Mt 18:20 MSG) In a very real way we encounter Jesus in and through each other. So come and check out our site. Make a friend! See my video: HopeforAllFellowship.com/Connect

Pray for unity of spirit among all believers however we may differ. Our oneness was at the core of Jesus' heart-wrenching prayer at the most critical moment of His life—the eve of His crucifixion. How telling! And why did He pray this? That the world may know God sent Him. He said everyone would know we are His disciples *by our love for one another*. Such love validates our witness *and* message. (Jn 17:11, 21-23; 13:35) Learn how Hope for All can help bring us together in love and purpose: HopeforAllFellowship.com/Connect

Hope for All Fellowship
PO Box 6271, Brownsville, TX 78523
Email: gerry@HopeforAllFellowship.com
(800) 254-1334 HopeforAllFellowship.com

About the Author

Gerry and his wife, Denise, have been married since 1980 and have three daughters and seven grandchildren. They've been involved in Christian missions since 1986, ordained in ministry in 1992.

They have lived and served overseas for many years—in Asia and Africa, serving with Youth With A Mission, Philippine Health Care Ministries, the Luke Society and Dakar Academy in Senegal, W. Africa. They helped pioneer the "House of Hope" in Senegal—a medical-dental health care clinic serving those in great need. It continues to this day.

Since 2001, Gerry has been training lay persons in simplified dental care for the developing world. Recently, he has adopted an exciting dental care breakthrough which enables him to train missionaries and international aid workers *both* online and in one and two-day workshops. www.DentalTrainingForMissions.com

Why write a book about eternal destiny?

Although Gerry believed in and loved God for most of his life, he was deeply troubled—troubled over the horrific teaching of everlasting punishment. He saw the contradictions this belief created in Scripture and in the Christian faith and sensed deep in his spirit that something was very wrong.

What qualifies Gerry to write such a book?

When a close friend, a pastor, shared this hope with him in 1998, Gerry was compelled to search it out for himself—being what some might call a Berean.[601] For many years he has intensively reflected on the works of others and studied the Scriptures on this theme. He has found solid Biblical evidence for his conclusion of hope—evidence that is here presented in simple terms most people can understand.

Gerry asked himself, "Who am I to write such a book?" Then he recalled 1 Corinthians 1:26-29:

"God hath chosen the foolish things of the world to confound the wise ... that no flesh should glory in His presence." (KJV)

Those words inspired him to the task of writing ... believing that God would indeed bless his endeavor.

Gerry shares part of his journey into this Hope in a short 6 minute YouTube video: www.youtube.com/watch?v=vJ07EnXaGos

Notes

[1] She is referring to my first book, *Hope Beyond Hell*.(a)
(a) Beauchemin, Gerry; with D. Scott Reichard. Hope Beyond Hell. Olmito: Malista Press, 2010.

[2] Barnes, Albert. "God is Worthy of Our Confidence." *Barnes' Practical Sermons*. Sermon VIII. *Bible Study Tools*. Biblical Repository for July, 1840. 123-125.
www.biblestudytools.com/sermons/barnes-practical-sermons/

[3] He preceded by saying: "This is a point on which we ought not long to dwell." I.e., he cautions us to not think too deeply on these difficult and perplexing questions. How revealing! I would say that if what we believe about the Gospel is true, its hope and joy will withstand all scrutiny and not be tarnished by deep thought. FYI: *Barnes' Notes* was one of the first Bible commentaries I purchased as a young believer back in the 1970s. I had no idea he had suffered such awful despair in his faith.

[4] David Konstan is a former John Rowe workman distinguished professor emeritus of classics and professor emeritus of comparative literature at Brown University among many other accomplishments. His research mainly focuses on ancient literature and classical philosophy.

[5] Mitchell, Jonathan. *The New Testament: God's Message ...* (Paperback) Amazon.

[6] www.BibleHub.com/interlinear/
www.scripture4all.org/OnlineInterlinear/Greek_Index.htm
www.archive.org/stream/interlinearliter00newy#page/492/mode/2up

[7] (Heb 6:19a NIV) This passage refers to God's all-inclusive promise to Abraham (v. 14) quoted from Gn 22:17-18, which orginates in Gn 12:1-3. See Anchor 1, "The Gospel to Abraham." Interestingly, Heb 6:19-20 concludes an NIV subsection titled "The Certainty of God's Promise."

[8] Most modern translations do not have the word "hell" anywhere in the Old Testament. For example: NIV, NIRV, NLV, VOICE, ERV, NET, ISV, ESV, ASV, NAS, RSV, NRSV, REB, NLT, AMP, LEB, NEB, MOUNCE, DBY, NCV, HCSB, PME, NAB, NABRE, 2001 T, TLV, CJB, etc. Though the word "hell" is absent, many think Dn 12:2 supports it: "And many of those who sleep in the dust of the earth shall awake, some to *everlasting* [*olām* H5769] life, some to shame and *everlasting* [*olām*] contempt." However, MYLT reads: "And the multitude of those sleeping in the dust of the ground do awake, some to life *age-during* and some to reproaches–to abhorrence *age-during*." As shown in Anchor 4, the meaning of *aiōnios* in Mt 25:46 applies equally with Dn 12:2, since *aiōnios* is the equivalent of *olām* in the Greek LXX. "Professor David Bentely Hart writes: "The Septuagint ... the Bible for much of the

early church, and which provides nine-tenths of all the quotations from the Hebrew scripture found in the NT—serves as something of a guide to how various expressions of the Jewish concept *olam* or *alma* were typically rendered in Greek (for instance, in Deuteronomy 15:17 *olam* is used to indicate the period of the life of a slave, and in the Septuagint version of that passage is rendered as *aiōn*)."[a] Numerous OT texts referring to *olām* show it cannot be endless in those texts. For example: Sodom's fiery judgment is *olām*—until God returns them to their former state. (Ez 16:53-55; Ju. 7) A Moabite is forbidden to enter the Lord's congregation *olām*—until the 10th generation. (De 23:3) A slave serves his master *olām*—until death ends his servitude. (Ex 21:6) The Mosaic covenant is *olām*—until it vanishes away. (Le 24:8; He 8:7-13) The priesthood is *olām*—until the likeness of Melchizedek arises. (Ex 40:15; Nu 25:13; He 7:14-22) Stones are to be a memorial *olām*—but where are they now? (Jos 4:7) Naaman's leprosy shall cling *olām*—but only until his death. (2K 5:27) God dwells in Solomon's temple *olām*—until it is destroyed. (2Ch 7:16; 1K 8:13; 9:3) Animal sacrifices were to be offered *olām*—until ended by Christ. (2Ch 2:4; He 7:11-10:18) Israel's judgment is *olām*—until the Spirit is poured out. (Is 32:13-15) Zion is an *olām* excellence—until many generations. (Is 60:15) For examples of G *aionios*, see Anchor 4—*The Greek Septuagint (LXX)*.

Finally, if Dn 12:2 did warn of an endless hell, consider the implications: (a) God waits 3,500 years after Adam to warn only a tiny fraction of humanity—the Jews. (b) Subsequently, the Jews are not commanded to warn other nations. (c) Of 23,145 verses in the OT, God chose only one verse to warn us of the worst penalty imaginable—while He devotes countless sections warning of temporal penalties. (d) Dn 12 is near the end of the OT where it takes an average Bible reader two years to come to (when using a three-year Bible reading plan). (e) Finally, relatively few people persevere in reading the Bible that far. My point is simple and conclusive: If endless punishment were true, a loving God would have warned of it everywhere in the Bible. In fact, He would not restrict Himself to the Bible at all. He would supernaturally warn every single person on earth—whether in a dream, by revelation, through angels or by whatever means is necessary.

[a] Hart, David Bentley. *The New Testament: A Translation*. New Haven: Yale University Press, 2017. 541.

[9] God knows the future: Gn 3:15; 15:13-14; Ex 3:19; 7:14; 9:30; 11:9; 1Kgs 13:1-6, 32; 21:20-22; 2Kgs 8:12; Ps 94:8-9; 139:1-6; 147:5; Is 41:21-26; 44:11, 21, 28; 46:9-11; 65:24; Jer 1:5; 32:19; Ez 11:5; Mt 6:8, 10; 10:17, 18, 21, 22; 11:14, 21; 12:45; 24:2, 33-41; Mk 14:30; Lk 14:28-32; Jn 6:64; 8:20; 21:18-19; Acts 2:23; 15:8, 18; 17:26; Rom 4:17; 8:29-30; 11:2, 33; Gal 3:8; Eph 1:4-5, 11; 3:11; 2Tm 1:9; Ti 1:2; Heb 4:13; 1Pt 1:2, 20; 1Jn 3:20; Rv 13:8; 17:18. Also see all Messianic prophecies.

[10] " ... you shall surely *die*." Gn 2:17; Rom 1:32

[11] "I will put enmity between you [evil powers] and the woman, and between your seed and her Seed [Jesus]; He shall bruise thy head [destroy evil] and thou shall bruise

[injure—not destroy] His heel [on the cross]." (Gn 3:15) This prophecy affirms Jesus' total victory over sin, death and all evil powers on our behalf. (Heb 2:14-15)

[12] "Also for Adam and his wife the Lord God made tunics of skin and clothed them." (Gn 3:21) Anthony Johnson wrote, "God's act of covering His disobedient children with skin, obtained through the shedding of blood, typifies Christ's redeeming sacrifice for them and all people (1Pt 1:18-19). It speaks of His once and for all covering, cleansing and removal of humanity's sin through the death of His Son (Jn 1:29)."[a]

[a] Johnson, Anthony. *The Larger Hope*. UK. Self-Published. 2014.

[13] I have heard this preached and read about it numerous times. The significance of being "clothed" by God is seen in texts such as Ephesians 4:24, Revelation 3:18 and 22:14 NAS.

[14] "'Whoever kills Cain, vengeance shall be taken on him sevenfold.' And the Lord set a mark on Cain, lest anyone finding him should kill him." (Gn 4:15)

[15] See 1Pt 3:19-20 and 4:6. Also Anchor 5, numbers 13-16.

[16] Vallowe, Ed F. "The Number Seven in the Holy Bible." *Biblical Mathematics*. Rainbow Bridge Ministries. 1998. www.angelfire.com/az/rainbowbridge/seven.html

[17] Note it says, "shall be" blessed, not "has the potential to be."

[18] Calvinism (Reformed theology) teaches:

> A. Because all have sinned, it is morally acceptable and just for God to punish human beings forever.
> B. However, because God is also merciful, He has sovereignly chosen to save a few from that horrific destiny through Jesus Christ.
> C. Those He elects to save are no more deserving of salvation than the rest of humanity.
> D. Their Gospel message is considered Good News because He at least saves some people from endless suffering.
> E. This theology, if truly believed, only leads to despair and anguish since we have no way of knowing for sure if our dearest loved ones or even ourselves are elected to salvation. It is especially heart-wrenching when you hear how "hell" is described by Jonathan Edwards. See note 20 below.

[19] Jonathan Edwards (1703-1758) is a famed American preacher, philosopher and theologian, perhaps the most renowned proponent of an eternal hell in the last three centuries. From "Discourses on Various Important Subjects," (1738).

[20] Jonathan Edwards partially describes hell this way: "Do but consider what it is to suffer extreme torment forever, and ever to suffer it day and night … from one year to another … one age to another … one thousand ages to another … in pain, in wailing and lamenting, groaning and shrieking … with your souls full of dreadful grief … your bodies and every member full of racking torture, without any possibility of getting ease … [or] moving God to pity by your cries … [or] diverting your thoughts from your pain. … After you shall have worn out a thousand more such ages, yet you shall have no

hope, but shall know that you are not one whit nearer to the end of your torments; but that still there are the same groans, the same shrieks, the same doleful cries ... which will not have been at all shortened by what shall have been past."[a]

Where is this God-defaming description of hell found in the Bible? This is merely the wild imagination of a darkened heart. How would Christ respond to such a person? He would rebuke them saying: "You do not know what manner of spirit you are of, for I did not come to destroy men's lives but to save them." (Lk 9:51-56)

[a] Edwards, Jonathan. "The Eternity of Hell Torments." *International Outreach, Inc.* Unedited version. 1750. www.jonathan-edwards.org.

[21] RSV, AMP, GNT, PME, NEB, JB

[22] RSV ("not sound"); JB, NET ("diseased"); EXB, NIV, NIVUK, NRSV ("unhealthy").

[23] Dt 15:9-11; Mk 7:21-23. Jesus said, "Is it not lawful for me to do what I wish with my own things? Or is your eye evil [envious-NAS] because I am good [generous-NAS]." (Mt 20:15; context 1-16) The earlier, and also envious workers in this parable despised God's generosity toward the latter workers; their selfish heart blinded them from seeing God's true goodness, perceiving it as injustice.

[24] John Piper, a contemporary proponent of Edwards,[a] in response to one anguished over the death of a loved one in hell says: "In the age to come we will be granted the emotional framework to *feel satisfaction* and *approval*."[b] Note his words "satisfaction" and "approval." Google: "Calvinism" and "Reformed Theology."

[a] Piper, John. "Thank You, Yale, For This Gift." *Desiring God.* 11 Feb 2009. www.desiringgod.org.

[b] Piper, John. "What Hope Can We Have for Lost Loved Ones?" *Desiring God.* 28 Dec 2007. www.desiringgod.org

[25] See also Dt 5:22; 7:9; Ex 20: 1-17; 31:18; 32:16; 34:6-7, 28.

[26] God is just and would not penalize a person for the sins of another. "The son will not bear the punishment for the father's iniquity." (Ez 18:19-20) See also Dt 24:16. It may mean that if children continue in the same sins as their parents, they too will reap the same consequences. Or, the negative traits and attitudes of parents rub off on their kids through several generations. Ex 34 CJB: "Causing [allowing] the negative effects of the parents' offenses to be experienced by their children." I trust the interpretation that harmonizes best with God's character.

[27] An LEB footnote states: "'Generations' is understood from comparison with parallel verses (compare Ex 34:6-7; Dt 7:9." See also the AMP, CEV, ERV, EXB, GW, GNT, HCSB, JUB, LEB, NOG, NET, NIV, NLT, TLV, VOICE. Mercy to thousands of generations is hyperbole meaning that God's mercy never ends. For example, see Psalm 136 where all 26 verses proclaim that God's mercy endures forever. See Anchor 8.

[28] See the CEB, GW, GNT, HCSB, NOG, NABRE, NLT, TLV which include of generations.

[29] "The Torah is Judaism's most important text. It is composed of the Five Books of Moses and ... contains the 613 commandments (*mitzvot*) and the Ten Commandment. ... The word "Torah" means "to teach."[a]
[a] Pelaia, Ariela. "What is the Torah? All About the Torah, Judaism's Imporant Text." *ThoughtCo.* 12 July 2017. www.judaism.about.com

[30] Erubin 19a

[31] Ariela Pelaia holds a masters degree from Jewish Theological. Seminary.
Pelaia, Ariela. "Does Judaism Believe in an Afterlife? What Happens After We Die?" *ThoughtCo.* 7 June 2017. www.judaism.about.com [a]
[a] Original source: Raphael, Simcha Paul. *Jewish Views of the Afterlife*. Northvale: Jason Aronson, Inc, 1996. Raphael is adjunct assistant prof. in Jewish Studies at Temple Univ., a spiritual director at Reconstructionist Rabbinical College.

[32] *Sheol* H7585, is translated "hell" 31times, "grave" 30 times, "pit" 3 times in the KJV. The Greek OT (LXX) translates the Hebrew *Sheol* as *Hades*.

[33] Beecher, Edward. *History of Opinions on the Scriptural Doctrine of Retribution*. New York: D. Appleton, 1878. Ch 27.

[34] Beecher, E. Ibid. www.tentmaker.org/books/Retribution/DoctrineOfRetribution.html

[35] See www.HopeForAllFellowship.com/EarlyChurch. For scholars: *The Christian Doctrine of Apokatastasis: A Critical Assessment from the New Testament to Eriugena (Supplements to Vigiliae Christianae)*. n.p.:BRILL, 2013. Ramelli, Ilaria Ph.D.

[36] Lk 14:26

[37] Tasker, R.V.G. *The Gospel According to St. Matthew*. Grand Rapids: Wm. B. Eerdmans Publishing Co., 1979. 240.

[38] Dt 4:20; Jer 11:4

[39] Nm 11:18

[40] Allin, Thomas. *Christ Triumphant*. Reprint 9th ed. Canyon Country: Concordant Publishing Concern, first published in England, 1890. Ch 9, 279-280.

[41] Errico, Rocco. *And There Was Light*. Smyrna: The Noohra Foundation, Inc., 1998. 9.

[42] Purcell, Boyd C. Ph. D. *Christianity Without Insanity*. CreateSpace Independent Publishing Platform. 2012. 77.

[43] Gavazonni, John. Email from a dear friend, a career minister and Bible teacher.

[44] Barclay, William. *The Gospel of Luke*. Daily Study Bible Series. Philadelphia: Westminster, 1978. 196.

[45] Mt 11:25; Mk 4:10-12, 33-34; Is 6:9-10; Lk 8:8-10; 24:45; Jn 16:25, 29; Ro 11:33.

[46] The fact the "righteous" dwell (can remain in company) with a God who is a devouring fire with everlasting burning affirms the positive purpose of His fiery nature.

[47] "Everything ... will be destroyed [or dissolved] by fire [heat; burning], and the earth and everything in it [or all the deeds done on it] will be exposed." (2Pt 3:10b EXB)

[48] Most theologians believe this passage refers to the lake of fire. See Question #26 for more on the lake of fire.

[49] 1Cor 13:8 RSV; see NRSV, ERV, ESV, EXB, GW, GNT, PME, LEB, TLB, MOUNCE, NOG, NCV, NET, NLV, WE, LB, TEV, JB, NEB.

[50] Mal 3:2-4, 6

[51] Gn 12:3; 18:18; 22:18; 26:4; 28:14; Acts 3:25-26; Gal 3:8

[52] S. Michael Houdmann writes: "The 'daughter of Zion' is mentioned several times in the [OT], usually in prophecy and once in poetry. 'Zion' meant Jerusalem and, later, Israel as the people of God. 'Daughter of Zion', then, does not refer to a specific person. It's a metaphor for Israel and the loving, caring, patient relationship God has with His chosen people."[a]

[a] Houdmann, S. Michael. "What does the Bible mean when it refers to a 'Daughter of Zion'?" www.gotquestions.org. Houdmann holds a master's degree in Christian Theology from Calvary Theological Seminary (Kansas City, MO).

[53] Good News Translation reads "purified."

[54] "For" (*gar* G1063) is "a causative particle standing always after one or more words in a clause ... expressing the reason for what has been before, affirmed or implied."[a] The NIV (along with others) leaves out this significant word.

[a] Zodhiates, Spiros. *The Complete Word Study Dictionary New Testament*. Iowa Falls: World Bible, 1992. 357.

[55] See Question #25: "What about the unquenchable fire?"

[56] "[Jesus] learned obedience by the things which He suffered." (Heb 5:8)

[57] Footnote from the NIV.

[58] New Living Translation

[59] *Sheol* H7585: translated "hell" 31times, "grave" 30 times, "pit" 3 times in the KJV.

[60] Ps 139:7-10

[61] Phil 2:13; 1Jn 4:17; 3:2; Eph 4:13; Heb 12:5-11

[62] Jas 1:17 NET; Mal 3:6

[63] Or justice. Both concepts support my point. BibleGateway lists 14 with "judgment."

[64] Gn 1:26-27; 9:6

[65] TNT

[66] "Through deceit they *refuse to know Me* ... therefore ... I will refine them and try them." (Jer 9:6-7) God's judgment towards unbelievers (those who refuse to know Him), is to refine them. Also, Peter wrote, "How true it is that God does not show favoritism but accepts from *every nation* the one [i.e., everyone] who fears him [venerates and has a reverential fear for God—AMP] and does what is right." (Acts 10:34-35 NIV) The lesson is that the loving principles governing God's judgments apply equally to everyone. He is not partial. See also: Nm 16:22; Ps 145:9; Rom 2:11; Gal 2:6; Eph 6:9; Col 3:25; 1Tm 2:3-4; 1Pt 1:17.

[67] The LXX uses recompense G467 in *both* clauses. Since it has become part of the inspired NT text (see note 110), we should ponder this in light of what Prof. Vincent says about vengeance: See notes 182, 475.

[68] All humanity receives pardon from our inherited sin in Adam through Christ's redemption as the last Adam. (Rom 5:11-21; 1Cor 15:22, 45; 1Jn 2:2) We gain "legal" pardon based solely on the merits of Christ just as we have legally inherited Adam's sin. Note that the legal, financial term involved is "redeem." (1Pt 1:18; Eph 1:7) Yet relational forgiveness depends on each individual's response to God's truth revealed in his or her heart. "To whom much is given (revealed), much is required." (Lk 12:48)

God is absolutely fair and just with each person. (Lv 24:19) "If we confess our sins, He is faithful and just to forgive us our sins and to cleanse us from all unrighteousness." (1Jn 1:9) This is "relational" forgiveness as it is linked to confession, a relational act. Notice the reason He forgives: He is "just." Why is this a factor? Because Christ has already paid the ransom for the sins of the whole world! (1Tm 2:6; 1Jn. 2:2) But that does not exclude God from doing it on His terms and for our correction. (Prv 3:11-12) Remember, He is a loving Father to all, as seen in Anchor 7.

[69] 1Cor 15:22

[70] "Though I ... understand all mysteries and ... I have all faith ... but have not love, I am nothing. And though I bestow all my goods to feed the poor, and though I give my body to be burned, but have not love, it profits me nothing." (1Cor 13:2-3) See also Mk 12:30-31; Rom 13:10; Gal 5:14; 6:2; Jas 2:8

[71] "Love has been perfected among us in this: that we may have boldness in the day of judgment; because as He is, so are we in this world." (1Jn 4:17)

[72] "For it is God who is at work within you, giving you the will and the power to achieve his purpose." (Phil 2:13 PME) See Phil 1:6; Eph 2:10; 1Jn 5:3.

[73] Do not misunderstand John 5:24 which says that those who hear Christ's word and believe in Him shall not come into judgment. John means that if we are hearing His word, i.e., are listening to it, giving heed to it, obeying it, we are not being judged, i.e., corrected, but we are walking in the life of God—the abundant life. (Jn 10:10) See these translations: JB, AMP, EXB, GW, TLB, NOG, NLT, MSG, NEB, William Barclay's commentary. The Bible is full of warnings to believers.

[74] Mt 25:35-36; Jas 1:27

[75] 1Cor 3:10-15

[76] Rv 20:4-6

[77] For example, in the parable of two servants in Matthew 24:51, the unfaithful servant is appointed "his portion" with the hypocrites where there will be weeping and gnashing of teeth. PME reads: "will punish him severely and send him off to share the penalty of the unfaithful—to his bitter sorrow and regret!" Nothing in this penalty requires us to think it is endless. "His portion" implies a defined, limited judgment.

Consider also: "For His anger is but for a moment, His favor is for life; weeping may endure for a night, but joy comes in the morning." (Ps 30:5) There is no judgment that endures beyond what our loving Father will permit for the good and restoration of His children.

[78] Phil 4:8

[79] Neh 8:10

[80] Egypt is the most mentioned nation in the Bible besides Israel. It is referred to, in its various forms, 857 times. Prof. Thayer writes, "Egypt has been called the 'Mother of Superstitions'... Greeks and Romans, Lawgivers and Philosophers ... freely credit her with the original invention of the fables and terrors of the invisible world ... It [endless punishment] was the common doctrine of Egypt, as all agree; and 'Moses was learned in all the wisdom of the Egyptians.' Acts 7: 22. And yet ... he never alludes to it."[a] Thayer explains that the Egyptians could not have inherited the idea of endless punishment from Israel's patriarchs since it was totally absent from the Law of Moses. Jon Sweeney, an author of medieval themes, explains, "It was the Italian poet Dante Alighieri who changed everything with his famous *Inferno* (1306+ CE). ... But to read the *Inferno* today is to realize how little it has to do with the Bible. There is more Greek and Roman mythology—adapted by Dante from classics such as Hesiod's *Theogony*, Virgil's *Aeneid*, and Ovid's *Metamorphoses*—than there is scripture in Dante's nine circles of hell.'"[b] See video: www.youtube.com/watch?v=j3WuSESO6EM&t=162s

[a] Thayer, Thomas B. "The Origin and History of the Doctrine of Endless Punishment." *Tentmaker*. Boston: UPH, 1855. www.tentmaker.org/books/OriginandHistory.html

[b] Sweeney, Jon M. *The Invention of Hell*. New York: Jericho Books Hachette Book Group, 2014. 3. www.youtube.com/watch?v=j3WuSESO6EM&t=162s

[81] For example: search Lk 16:23 at www.Biblegateway.com. Most translations do not translate *Hades* as "hell." *Sheol* defined: www.biblestudytools.com/dictionary/sheol/

[82] Further in this chapter, the significance of the LXX is discussed.

[83] The Apostle Paul quotes from this passage, in 1Cor 15:55, affirming its victory. He attests to the glorious and positive translation of this passage as a statement of fact. This is confirmed in the last clause of Hosea 13:14: "Where is your sting O *Hades*?"

[84] The ancient Greek manuscript, the *Textus Receptus*, on which the KJV and NKJV are based, reads *Hades*. The NKJV says it accurately: "O *Hades*, where is your victory?" I realize that most other translations are based on different Greek texts (Received and Westcott) which twice in the second clause, reads "O death" (*thanatos*) not *Hades*. But this is a direct quote from Hosea 13:14 and the Greek Septuagint accurately translates it *Hades*. This affirms that the *Textus Receptus*, at least in this case, shows the more accurate rendering of this passage. In addition, the context (vs. 15:51-57) affirms total victory in Christ over death, which would of course include *Hades*. Paul attests to the glorious and positive translation of this passage as a statement of fact in 1Cor 15:55, where he quotes the last clause of Hosea 13:14: "Where is your sting O *Hades*?"

[85] See the KJV translator's official guidelines #1 and #4.[a]

[a] Hall, Isaac H., ed., "History of the King James Version." See guidelines at: www.bible-researcher.com/kjvhist.html

[86] Neither has Paul ever used the Greek word *Gehenna*—translated "hell" in most English Bibles.

[87] This is especially so, since we frequently hear evangelists say when explaining the Gospel that if "you" (the hearer) were the only person that ever lived, Christ would still have died for you.

[88] Lk 4:18-19; 1Pt 3:19; 4:6—See Anchor 5, examples 13-16.

[89] See Anchor 6, "The Written Law."

[90] "*Gehenna* was a real place . . . the Jerusalem rubbish dump, and was just outside the city. Smoke went up from it at all times as the rubbish was burning continually. It was full of maggots, and the bodies of the worst criminals were thrown there. Josiah used it for the burning of offal. It used to be the site of child sacrifice to Molech."[a] Some have noted that today the location of *Gehenna* is a green city park.

[a] Nyland, Dr. A. *The Source New Testament*. Australia: Smith & Stirling, 2007. 23.

[91] Renowned early American theologian.

[92] However, Edwards claims the last cent deserves infinite punishment and thus can never be paid.[a] This contradicts the words of Jesus, and even worse, it dishonors Him by implying that He raises false hopes with deceptive words.

[a] Jonathan Edwards, from his sermon, "The Eternity of Hell Torments." Section III. April 1739.

[93] Dr. David Crump claims that the wealth of literature dealing with this sermon is *overwhelming*.[a]

[a] Crump, David. "Applying The Sermon On The Mount: Once You Have Read It What Do You Do With It?" *Criswell Theological Review 6.1*. The Criswell College, 1992. 13-14. www.faculty.gordon.edu.

[94] Gal 3:24

[95] As we see throughout the chapter, these were the scribes and Pharisees whom Jesus rebuked, guilty of all the righteous blood that has been shed against God's Holy Prophets (v. 35) of whom Jesus is the pinnacle.

[96] The Good News Translation reads "purified."

[97] See Anchor 2, "Fire Transforms," *"Fire Purifies."*

[98] Jer 31:40. For scholarly support that this valley relates to *Gehenna*, see: "Expansion of Jerusalem in Je 31;38-40," by Dennis M. Swanson M.Div., *The Master's Seminary Journal*. TMSJ 17/1 (Spr 2006) 17-34. www.tms.edu/m/17b.pdf.

[99] Hart, David Bentley. *The New Testament: A Translation*. New Haven: Yale University Press, 2017. 543-548. Amazon.

[100] *The Emphasized Bible.* 1902. Also referred to as Rotherham's Emphasized Bible (REB). Read free online. Amazon Kindle. www.archive.org/stream/RotherhamEmphasizedBible/Rotherham_Emphasized_Bible#page/n9/mode/2up

[101] *Concordant Literal New Testament*: with Keyword Concordance. 6th Ed., 1983.

[102] *The New Testament: God's Message ...* by Jonathan Paul Mitchell. 2010. Amazon.

[103] *The Source New Testament:* with Extensive Notes on Greek .... 2007. Amazon.

[104] *Modern Young's Literal Translation New Testament.* 2005. Amazon or Read original YLT free online at www.biblegateway.com

[105] *The Twentieth Century New Testament* (1904) Amazon or Read free online: www.biblestudytools.com/wnt/

[106] *Weymouth New Testament* (or *New Testament in Modern Speech*) (1903) Amazon. or Read free online: www.biblestudytools.com/wnt/

[107] *Far Above All Bible Translation* (2009-2011) www.faraboveall.com/050_BibleTranslation/01_BibleTranslationIndex.html
A free download: www.biblesupport.com/e-sword-downloads/file/7094-far-above-all-nt-literal-translation/

[108] *The 2001 Translation* (2001) Read free online: www.2001translation.com/

[109] *The New Testament: A Translation* (2017) Amazon.

[110] Hart, David Bentley. The New Testament: A Translation. New Haven: Yale University Press, 2017. 541, cp 537-543.
In addition, Paul Lawrence writes, "The 'Septuagint' was the first translation of any part of the Hebrew Bible into another language, so its place in world history is assured. Furthermore, its use as the version of the OT most frequently used by the writers of the NT only serves to further enhance its significance."[a]
[a] Lawrence, Paul, PhD. "A Brief History of the Septuagint." *Associates for Biblical Research*. 31 Mar 2016. www.biblearchaeology.org

[111] Based on the Greek Septuagint LXX, ABP. www.septuagint-interlinear-greek-bible.com/ Reference *aiōnios* G166.

[112] Vincent, Marvin. *Word Studies in the New Testament*. Vol. IV, 1887. Grand Rapids: Eerdmans, 1973. 58-59, 291.

[113] Mt 25:46; 18:8-9; 25:41; 2Thes 1:9; Heb 6:2

[114] Augustine, a renowned leader of the early church in the fifth century, admitted he knew little of the Greek language. *The Enchiridion*, Sec.112.

[115] Beecher, Edward. *History of Opinions on the Scriptural Doctrine of Retribution. Tentmaker.* New York: D. Appleton, 1878. Ch 19-20. www.tentmaker.org

[116] Anderson, Michael H. MDiv. "The Apostle's Creed." *Creeds of Christendom.* www.creeds.net. (PME)

[117] Anderson, Michael H. MDiv. "The Nicene Creed." *Creeds of Christendom.* www.creeds.net. (International Consultation on English Texts translation).

[118] Beecher, Edward. Ibid.
Dr. Marcellino D'Ambrosio confirms that the Apostles' Creed predated the Nicene: "The Apostles' Creed originally came from the baptismal ceremony of the Church of Rome, founded by the great apostles Peter and Paul. ... The Creed we call "Nicene" was expanded by the first two ecumenical councils ... to emphasize the equality of Jesus with the Father and the divinity of the Holy Spirit. The Apostles Creed underwent no such official expansion."[a]

[a] D'Ambrosio, Marcellino, PhD. "The Apostles Creed & The Nicene Creed." *Crossroads Initiative.* 17 Oct 2016. www.crossroadsinitiative.com

[119] If there had been a consensus among the early fathers that endless punishment was the doom of all sinners, they would surely have warned of it in their creeds. The fact that no reference to it is made, reveals that these Greek-speaking fathers did not, as a community, believe that doctrine. As native Greek speakers, they knew the true meaning of *aiōnios*.

[120] The CLT reads: "in accord with the revelation of a secret hushed in times eonian [*aiōnios* G166], yet manifested now ... according to the injunction of the eonian [*aiōnios* G166] God." See Greek-English interlinear translation: www.Scripture4all.org for further confirmation: www.scripture4all.org/OnlineInterlinear/NTpdf/rom16.pdf

[121] See ABP: www.septuagint-interlinear-greek-bible.com. Compare with Is 40:4.

[122] Is 40:4

[123] ABP: www.septuagint-interlinear-greek-bible.com

[124] Vincent, M. Ibid. Vol. IV. 58-59. More: www.HopeForAllFellowship.com/phemail

[125] "Jonah was in the belly of the fish *three days and three nights."* (Jn 1:17) Yet, Jonah said, "I went down to the moorings of the mountains; the earth with its bars closed behind me *forever* [*aiōnios*—ABP-LXX]; Yet You have brought up my life from the pit, O Lord, my God." (Jon 2:6)

[126] Konstan, David, and Ilaria Ramelli. *Terms for Eternity.* First Ed. Piscataway: Gorgias Press, 2007. 238. Konstan is prof. of classics & comparative lit. at Brown Univ. Ramelli, assist. prof. ancient philosophy, Catholic U. of Milan.

[127] Tasker, R.V.G., gen. ed., *The Tyndale New Testament Commentaries: The Gospel According to St. Matthew. An Introduction and Commentary.* Grand Rapids: Wm. B. Eerdmans, 1961. 240. Tasker was also professor of NT Exegesis Univ. of London.

[128] David Bentley Hart was previously a professor at the Christian Studies Center. Hart has held the visiting Robert J. Randall Chair in Christian Culture at Providence College and visiting Danforth Chair in Theological Studies at St. Louis Univ.; he was also a fellow at the Univ. of Notre Dame's Institute for Advanced Study. He has taught at the Univ. of Virginia, the Univ. of St. Thomas, Duke Div.School and Loyola College. He is

the author of numerous books, including: *Atheist Delusions: The Christian Revolution and its Fashionable Enemies* (2009) and *The Beauty of the Infinite: The Aesthetics of Christian Truth* (2003). Hart earned his B.A. from the Univ. of Maryland, M.Phil. from the Univ.of Cambridge, and M.A. and Ph.D. from the Univ.of Virginia. www.berkleycenter.georgetown.edu/people/david-bentley-hart.

[129] Hart, David Bentley. The New Testament: A Translation. New Haven: Yale University Press, 2017. 537.

[130] Hart, David Bentley. Ibid. 543.

[131] Keizer, Heleen M. *Life, Time, Entirety – A Study of "AIŌN" in Greek Literature and Philosophy, the Septuagint and Philo.* Doctoral dissertation Univ. of Amsterdam, 1999. Slightly amended version, 2005. Chapter VI, Sec. I. 241. Should you think the adjective *aiōnios* differs in meaning from the noun, Dr. Keizer explains: "The stereotyped rendering of '*olām* by *aiōn* or *aiōnios* in the LXX entails that the Biblical word *aiōn(ios)* should be interpreted along the lines of '*olām*, not along the lines of non-Biblical, 'secular' Greek *aiōn(ios)*. ... In the LXX, *aiōn* is thus the standing representative of '*olām.*'" (p. 194) "The Hebrew expression '*olām-and-'ad* is rendered in the LXX by '*the aiōn and still/beyond*' and '(*the aiōn and*) the *aiōn of the aiōn.*' These Greek renderings, more explicitly even than the Hebrew original, reveal that the Biblical word *aiōn* ('*olām*) is not, as such, to be considered an ultimate term." Ibid. page 195. This work is available free as a PDF. Email us for a copy.

[132] Barclay, William. *A Spiritual Autobiography*. Grand Rapids: Eerdmans, 1977. 65-7.

[133] Email 10/ 5/ 2017. More: www.HopeForAllFellowship.com/phemail. Peter is senior pastor of *The Sanctuary Downtown*, Denver. He presents an understanding of fire and *aionios* worthy of serious consideration. See his book's Appendix: [a]

[a] Hiett, Peter. *The History of Time and the Genesis of You*. n.p. Relentless Love Publishing, 2015. Visit www.Relentess-Love.org

[134] Barclay, William. Ibid.

[135] www.blueletterbible.org/lang/lexicon/lexicon.cfm?Strongs=G2851&t=NASB

[136] Hart, David Bentley. Ibid. 53. Hart continues: "The verbal form, (kolazō), appears twice: in Acts 4:21 where it clearly refers only to disciplinary punishment, and in 2 Peter 2:9 in references to fallen angels and unrighteous men, where it probably means 'being held in check' or 'penned in' [until the day of judgment][a]."

The Jerusalem Bible reads, "Love *will come* to its perfection in us *when* we can face the day of Judgment without fear; [with fearless confidence[b]] because even in this world we have *become* as he is. In love there can be no fear, but fear is driven out by perfect love: because to fear is to expect punishment [*kolasis*] and anyone who is afraid is *still* imperfect in love." (1Jn 4:17-18)

Kolasis implies correction, since those who lack love are *still* imperfect in love. "*Still* imperfect" means perfect love has not *yet* been attained, but is in the process of it. Note these time words: "will come," "when," "become," and "still." Perfect love is attained over time; we are not born with it. And even when *kolasis* is translated punishment, it does *not* negate correction. Think about this: If we believed an eternal hell awaited us if we failed to attain perfect love, could we ever have true peace? Of course not! And since peace is central to life in Christ, endless punishment cannot be true.

(a) Hart's original brackets.

(b) "Without fear" is *parrēsia* G3954 which Dr. Thayer defines as "free and fearless confidence, cheerful courage, boldness, assurance." The NAS reads "have confidence."

[137] Since punishment, meted out in our human courts, is *both* retributive and remedial, I cannot imagine our Creator and Father doing any less.

[138] Hart, David Bentley. Ibid. 542.

[139] "Where *aiōnios* is used of that which is by nature eternal, God in himself, it certainly carries the connotation that, say, the English words 'enduring' or 'abiding' would do in the same context: *ever*lasting."[a]

[a] Hart, David Bentley. Ibid. 538.

[140] Regarding the pronoun "Him" in most translations, the context and wording imply that Christ is the subject. That is confirmed by these translations which specifically state "Jesus." ERV; EXB; GNT; NCV; NIRV

[141] *Modern Young's Literal Translation* (G *eis tous aiōnas tōn aiōnōn*)

[142] "Then comes the end, when He [Christ] *hands over* the kingdom to the God and Father, when He has abolished all rule and all authority and power. For He must reign *until* He has put all His enemies under His feet. ... When all things are subjected to Him, then the Son Himself [as Son of Man—our representative head] also will be subjected to the One who subjected all things to Him, so that God may be *all* in *all.*" (1Cor 15:25-28 NAS) Christ reigns "until," not for all eternity. There will come a time when He *hands over* His kingdom to His Father.

[143] *Modern Young's Literal Translation* (G *eis tous aiōnas tōn aiōnōn*)

[144] Paul affirms that Christ's faithful followers will co-reign with Him: 2Tm 2:12

[145] It was not people (dead in sin through Adam—like all human beings) that were totally annihilated. It was "such great riches that came to nothing, a city made desolate"—a corrupt social entity (city) that needed to be prevented from contaminating other communities, cities and nations. The citizens who died had no less hope than the people who drowned in Noah's day—to whom Christ brought Good News (1Pet 4:6) or those of Sodom and her daughters who will be given back [restored] the good things they once had [their fortunes]. (Eze 16:53 EXB)

[146] Though the phrase, "lake of fire" is not used here, most theologians assume it. See Question #26.

[147] Rv 14:10-11 (The New Testament: A Translation) Other translations say: "to ages of ages" (MYLT), "unto ages of ages" (REB), "until the ages of the ages" (Weymouth NT), "into the eons of eons" (ABP; also CLT and Greek Interlinear Bible).

[148] Translator David Bentley Hart, comments, "Everywhere else in Revelation, when John is speaking of final or everlasting things, he employs the standard phrase (*eis tous aiōnas tōn aiōnōn*), with the definite articles: "unto *the* ages of *the* ages." Here alone the articles are omitted, perhaps producing a weaker and more indefinite formula, one that might be read as meaning "for a very long time.""[a]

[a] Ibid. 518. Footnote af.

[149] See Anchor 6.

[150] How tragic that our tradition's teaching of endless punishment has led most translators to read that horrific idea into these judgment warnings. Jesus warned of invalidating the word of God (His "all" promises for example) for the sake of tradition. (Mt 15:6 NAS, also verses 3, 9)

[151] The "ages" (plural) of God's acts in human history are a mystery we cannot fully grasp, but are very real. "By *revelation* He made known to me the *mystery* ... which in *other ages was not made known* to the sons of men, *as it has now been revealed* by the Spirit to His holy apostles and prophets." (Eph 3:3-5) Professor Vincent writes, "In the NT the history of the world is conceived as developed through a succession of aeons. A series of such aeons precedes the introduction of a new series inaugurated by the Christian dispensation, and the end of the world and the second coming of Christ are to mark the beginning of another series. See Eph iii.11. Paul contemplates aeons before and after the Christian era. Eph i.21; ii.7; iii.9, 21; 1Cor x.11; comp. Heb ix. 26. He includes the series of aeons in one great aeon, *the aeon of the aeons* (Eph iii.21); and the author of the Epistle to the Hebrews describes the throne of God as enduring unto the aeon of the aeons (Heb i. 8). The plural is also used, *aeons of the aeons*, signifying all the successive periods which make up the sum total of the ages collectively. Rom xvi.27; Gal i.5; Phil iv.20,etc. This plural phrase is applied by Paul to God only."[a]

[a] Vincent, Marvin. Ibid. IV. 59.

[152] The TNT reads: "to the end that within the continuously oncoming ages He may exhibit (display; point out; give proof of)." See: CJB; DARBY; HCSB; ISV; AMP; DLNT; GNT; MOUNCE; NET

[153] See Anchor 10, "Hope in the Book of Revelation."

[154] Though water (life) cannot be gathered up again, it is not so with God. "*But God ...*" No situation is hopeless with God. Nothing is impossible with Him. (Lk 1:37) He has devised a way for the banished one to be restored—spilled water will be gathered up again.

[155] "His name [is] JESUS, for He will save His people from their sins." (Mt 1:21)

[156] Jn 10:11; Lk 19:10

[157] Our Good Shepherd expects us to seek our lost sheep until we find them; certainly He does no less for His (Lk 15:4-7).

[158] He came to heal the brokenhearted, proclaim liberty to the captives, set the oppressed free and comfort all who mourn. (Lk 4:18; Is 61:1-3)

[159] Barclay, William [renowned Greek scholar]. *The Letters to the Corinthians*. The Daily Study Bible Series. Philadelphia: Westminster, 1975. 153.

[160] "*Every* sin and blasphemy will be forgiven men, but the blasphemy against the Spirit will not be forgiven men ... either in this age or in the age to come." (Mt 12:31-32)

[161] Luke 20:35 shows that the age to come is the resurrection age. This does not say there is no forgiveness for blasphemy in a subsequent age, for Paul spoke of the "ages" to come. (Eph 2:7) See Question #20. The main point is that Jesus said sins will be forgiven in the coming ages. That undeniably affirms hope beyond death.

[162] Jn 4:42; 1Jn 4:14; Jn 12:47; 1Tm 4:10; Heb 13:8

[163] This is part of an extended discussion which concludes with verse 4:6. See also Lk 4:18; Is 61:1-2; Eph 4:8-10.

[164] Mt 5:22-26 as explained in Anchor 4, "Greek *Gehenna*," Point 1.

[165] www.xenos.org/essays/grammatical-historical-hermeneutics-lay-readers [a] Caution: This is only reliable *if* we know God's true character. Anchor 1: "Lamp of the Body"
[a] Willems, Kurt. "It Makes Plain Sense! Or So I Was Taught. ... " *Patheos*. 31 Jan 2012. www.patheos.com.

[166] Justin Martyr was a famous church father and defender of the faith who lived in the second century (100–165 AD).

[167] Barclay, William. Ibid. 242

[168] Barclay, William. *Letters of James and Peter*. Daily Study Bible Series. Philadelphia: Westminster, 1978. 248-9. More: www.HopeForAllFellowship.com/1Pt4.6

[169] Heath Bradley notes: "The NIV Study Bible acknowledges that translators added the word 'now' which isn't originally in this text. They reason that it is necessary to add this word so that the verse doesn't have the impression of allowing for opportunities for salvation in the afterlife, which is clearly wrong in their view. On this interpretation, the people preached to were alive, but now they are dead. This is simply a case where a prior theological conviction not only distorts the interpretation of a text, but it actually leads translators to add a word in order to make it say what they think it should say. Of course the Bible doesn't offer us the hope for salvation in the afterlife if verses that point in that direction are changed!"[a] See Scripture4All Interlinear: 1Peter 4.[b]
[a] Bradley, Heath. *Flames of Love*. Eugene: Wipf & Stock, 2012. 90; f.n. 20.
[b] www.scripture4all.org/OnlineInterlinear/NTpdf/1pe4.pdf

[170] He writes: "Archbishop Hilarion Alfeyev argues persuasively that the majority of the Eastern fathers embraced this interpretation. See Alfeyev's 'Christ the Conqueror of Hell,' 43-81."[a] Alfeyev holds a doctorate in philosophy from Oxford University and a doctorate in theology from St Sergius Orthodox Theological Institute in Paris.
[a] Bradley, Heath. Ibid. 91-92.

[171] Bradley, Heath. Ibid. 92.

[172] The Apostles' Creed reads: "[Christ] was crucified, dead, and buried. *He descended into hell* [*Hades*]: the third day he rose again from the dead."[a] Sadly this has been deleted in many modern editions of this creed. Regarding this clause, William Barclay says its first actual appearance, as a creedal statement, is in the Symbol of Sirmium in A.D. 359/60. But then he says, it was part of the Church's belief long before that. He quotes early church Father Irenaeus (130-203 AD), "The Lord descended into the regions beneath the earth, preaching his advent there also, and declaring the remission of sins." Barclay asserts that the original word is *Hades*—"*the place of the dead.*".[b]

[a] Anderson, Michael H. MDiv. "The Apostle's Creed." *Creeds of Christendom*. www.creeds.net. (PME)

[b] Barclay, William. *The Plain Man Looks at The Apostles' Creed*. London: Collins Press, 1967. 120-122, 127.

[173] Bradley, Heath. Ibid. 93.

[174] Barclay, William. Ibid. 242-243. More: www.HopeForAllFellowship.com/Creeds

[175] Heb 2:15; Mt 5:25, 1Pt 3:19

[176] Prof. Marvin Vincent defines "the lower parts of the earth" as "the underworld."[a] The reference is to Christ's descent into *Hades*. See Acts 2:27-31; Phil 2:10; Rv 5:13

[a] Vincent, Marvin. Ibid. Vol. III. 389.

[177] See also: Rom 8:13b; 2Cor 4:11; Eph 2:1; Col 3:3-5; 1Tm 5:6

[178] "All who are in the tombs will hear His voice, and will come forth; those who did the good deeds to a resurrection of life, those who committed the evil deeds to a resurrection of judgment." (Jn 5:28-29 NAS)

[179] And we know the blameless are not annihilated, since they inherit good (Prv 28:10).

[180] Jn 5:29

[181] Rom 11:26

[182] Jude 7. The CLT reads: "Sodom ... a specimen, experiencing the *justice* of fire eonian." Recall the limited duration of *aionios* as explained in Anchor 4. The MYLT reads, "Sodom ... an example, of fire age-during, *justice* suffering." Also, the word "vengeance" in many translations has no Greek support. Professor Marvin Vincent writes, "RSV [and most translations I have seen] rightly substitutes punishment for vengeance, since *dikē* G1349 carries the underlying idea of right or justice, which is not necessarily implied in the word 'vengeance.'"[a] *Dikē* is defined: justice (the principle, a decision, or its execution).[b] God will resurrect, judge (i.e., discipline and correct) and restore each inhabitant of Sodom.

[a] Vincent, Marvin. Ibid. Vol. I. 715.

[b] Strong, James. *New Strong's Concise Dictionary of the Words in the Greek Testament*. Nashville: Thomas Nelson, 1995. 24.

[183] See Anchor 6, "The Written Law."

[184] Jer 48:4, 42, 47; 49:2-6, 37-39

[185] Jer 18:3-6 NAS. Compare with Rom 8:21-22 and Rv 21:5.

[186] *Apōleia* is a presumed derivative of *apollumi* G622.
Strong, James. Ibid. 12.

[187] Professor Marvin Vincent wrote: "*olethros* does not always mean destruction or extinction.
Vincent, Marvin. Ibid. Vol. IV. 61.

[188] Vine, W. E. *An Expository Dictionary of Biblical Words.* Nashville: Nelson, 1985. 164.

[189] As seen in Anchor 6. Note: we "must *all* appear before the judgment seat of Christ." (2Cor 5:10) This is not annihilation, but physical death. Furthermore, the preceding verse states, "There is no partiality with God." (Rom 2:11)

[190] Mt 16:24; Mk 8:34-35; Lk 9:23

[191] Rom chapter 6, esp. 6:3. Rom 8:13; 12:1-2; 2Cor 4:11, 16; 5:15; Gal 2:20; Phil 3:10; 2Tm 2:11; Heb 5:7-9; 1Pt 2:21, 24; 1Jn 3:16. Also Mk 8:34; Jn 12:24-25; 15:4-5; 2Pt 1:3-12.

[192] Mt 10:6. Compare Rom 11:26, 32-33, 36.

[193] For example: Is 54:8; Jer 23:3; 32:36-42; Hos 14:4-7; Am 9:11-15.

[194] From a sermon given by Jonathan Edwards in 1739 titled "The Eternity of Hell Torments," Section I.

[195] Acts 4:27-30

[196] Heb 1:3 NAS

[197] Jn 14:9

[198] Lk 23: 39-43

[199] "Declaring the end from the beginning, and from ancient times things that are not yet done, saying, 'My counsel shall stand, and I will do all My pleasure.'" (Is 46:10)

[200] Bradley, Heath. Ibid. 18-19.

[201] The Source New Testament (SNT)

[202] Rv 15:3-4

[203] Mt 5:38-48

[204] 1Jn 4:8, 16

[205] Barclay, William. *The Gospel of Matthew.* Vol. 1. The Daily Study Bible Series. Philadelphia: Westminster, 1975. 163-165.

[206] Mt 5:38-48; Gal 5:14, 18, 22; 6:2; Rom 13:10; Jas 2:8

[207] Yet, the heart of Jesus is to bring us up to a higher plane than retributive justice, to unconditional love and mercy.

[208] Also Mt 5:17-18, 22-26, 38-48; Mk 4:24; Lk 6:38; Rv 18:7

[209] "He who does wrong will be *repaid* for what he has done, and there is no partiality." (Col 3:25; Rom 2:11)
"*Every* transgression and disobedience received a *just* penalty." (Heb 2:2 NAS)
"You will not get out of there [hell's prison] *until* you have paid the last penny." (Mt 5:26)
"Deliver him ... *until* he should pay all that was due. So my heavenly Father will do to you." (Mt 18:34-35)
"You will not depart from there *until* you have paid the very last cent." (Lk 12:59)
He who did a greater crime received *many* lashes, while the other received *few*. (Lk 12:45-48)
"He who sows sparingly will also reap *sparingly* ... sows bountifully will also reap *bountifully*." (2Cor 9:6)
"With the *same measure* you use it will be *measured* to you." (Mk 4:24)
"With the *same measure* that you use, it will be *measured* back to you." (Lk 6:38)
"Whatever a man sows that he will also reap." (Gal 6:7)
"Whatever good anyone does, he will receive the *same* from the Lord." (Eph 6:8)
"He who does wrong will be *repaid* for what he has done, and there is no partiality." (Col 3:25)
"Render to her just as she rendered to you ... according to her works." (Rv 18:6)
"In the *measure* that she ... lived luxuriously, in the *same measure* give her torment and sorrow." (Rv 18:7)
There are many more such passages throughout the Bible.

[210] Rv 20:12-15. For more on the lake of fire, see Anchor 2 and 10. Also Question #26.

[211] Verses 21:1-8 show that the sinners "outside" the Holy City are having their "part" in the lake of fire. Note: there are two domains in view—a Holy City and a lake of fire. The lake is alluded to as being just "outside" the city. (Rv 21:1-8; 22:14-15) Whether these are literal or metaphorical places is irrelevant—the spiritual reality they represent is the main issue. For more on the lake of fire, see Anchor 2 and 10. Also Question #26.

[212] Beauchemin, Gerry; with D. Scott Reichard. "The Trilogy" (addendum). *Hope Beyond Hell*. Olmito, TX: Malista Press, 2010. 243.

[213] Read more: *The Trilogy*. www.HopeForAllFellowship.com/Trilogy

[214] See the first two chapters of *Mere Christianity*. Lewis, C.S. Harper Collins Publishers. New York: 1952. Ch 1, 2.

[215] Also, note the role our love and heart (conscience) play in our assurance of and confidence in our faith in 1Jn 3:16-21; 4:17-18.

[216] For example: "The heart is more deceitful than all else and is desperately *sick.*" (Jer 17:9 NAS) Note! The KJV mentions *wicked* 491 times, but only *once* (Jer 17:9) is it based on *ânash* H605! This confirms why we must diligently compare translations.

[217] Strong, James. Ibid. 11. H605.

[218] The Greek Septuagint is a reliable authority for determining Biblical truth. See Anchor 4, Greek *Aionios*, "The Greek Septuagint (LXX)."

[219] *The New English Translation of the Septuagint,* and similarly, the ABP. LXX reads: "The heart is deep beyond all things, and man is, who shall know him? I the Lord am examining hearts."

[220] The Apostle Paul confirmed this: Rom 1:18, 19, 32; 2:14-16.

[221] Gn 1:26-27; 9:6

[222] See also: Rom 1:28-32; 2:1-2.

[223] "For" (*gär* G1063) is not always indicated in our translations (i.e., NIV, KJV, etc.) Yet others do (MYLT, CLT, NAS). Compare with Anchor 4, Greek *Gehenna*, #1.

[224] See also: Is 29:13. The context of this warning is related to the worship of God! Isaiah said their worship is merely lip service and not from the heart, because their fear of God is taught by the commandment (traditions) of men! What greater fear is there than that of an eternal hell? What removes one's heart further from God?

[225] Jn 1:1-3, 9, 14

[226] *The Bible Knowledge Commentary.* 1983. 340.

[227] "For God did not send his Son into the world to condemn the world, but to *save the world* through him." (Jn 3:17 NIV) "For I did not come to judge the world, but to save the world." (Jn 12:47) Jn 4:42; 1Jn 4:14

[228] Moses instructed: "Aaron shall lay both his hands on the head of the live goat, confess over it *all the iniquities* of the *children of Israel*, and *all their transgressions*, concerning *all their sins*, putting them on the head of the goat, and shall send it away into the wilderness. ... [It] shall bear on itself *all their iniquities* to an uninhabited land; and he shall release the goat in the wilderness."(Lv 16:21-22) This is repeated in this chapter. See verses 15-17, 19, 24, 30, 32, 33.

[229] Jn 17:4

[230] Is 53:6, 11; See also Jn 12:32, 33.

[231] Lk 15:1-10; 11-32; Mt 18:10-14

[232] Lk 18:9-14; Mt 5: 22-26; 2Cor 5:10, etc.; Cf. Mt 5:7 with Jas 2:13. See Anchor 3, "Synergism of Judgment with Mercy.*"*

[233] See Question #5. Christ died for people, not things. (Heb 2:9; 1Jn 2:2)

[234] See Anchor 3, "Synergism of Judgment with Mercy."

[235] Allin, Thomas. Ibid. 173.

[236] Anderson, Michael H. MDiv. Ibid.

[237] Anderson, Michael H. MDiv. "The Nicene Creed." *Creeds of Christendom.* www.creeds.net. (International Consultation on English Texts translation).

[238] Mt 10:5-7; 15:23-25

[239] Gn 12:2-3; See Anchor 9, Promise 3.

[240] Mt 5: 14-16; 28:19-20

[241] There is no favoritism with God. See Anchor 8, "No Favoritism."

[242] Statistics taken from *Baker's Evangelical Dictionary of Biblical Theology*[(a)] and *Strong's Concordance.*

[(a)] www.biblestudytools.com/dictionaries/bakers-evangelical-dictionary/

[243] Mt 5:16, 45, 48; 6:1, 4, 6, 8-9, 14-15, 18, 26, 32; 7:11-12

[244] See also Mt 4:23; 5:1-2.

[245] Mt 4:23; 5:1-2: Note the word "and" (*de* G1161—conjunction) which directly links verse 4:25 with 5:1. Note also that there are no chapter or paragraph breaks in the Greek text.[(a)] It does not matter that the cities and regions mentioned are found in the "territory" of Israel, as certainly not all Israelites were true believers, walking with and serving the God of Abraham, Isaac and Jacob, i.e., of Israel. "For they are not all Israel who are of Israel, *nor are they all children* because they are the seed of Abraham." (Rom 9:6-7)

[(a)] www.blueletterbible.org/lang/lexicon/lexicon.cfm?Strongs=G1161&t=NKJV

[246] Most translations say "offspring" which is defined as "children; descendant(s)."[(a)] Many translations specifically say "children." For example: TEV, NIV (1973), PME, JB, CJB, CEV, EXB, GW, ISV, NOG, VOICE, LB (Sons), TLB (Sons of God), TNT (Family).

[(a)] *Oxford American Desk Dictionary and Thesaurus.* Second Ed. New York: Berkley, 2001. 573.

[247] Rom 8:15, 23; 9:4; Gal 4:5; Eph 1:5

[248] Vine, W. E. Ibid. Section II, 13-14.

[249] Vincent continues, "Mr. Merivale, illustrating Paul's acquaintance with Roman law, says: 'The process of legal adoption by which the chosen heir became entitled not only to the reversion of the property but to the civil status, to the burdens as well as the rights of the adopter – became, as it were, his other self, one with him. ... We have but a faint conception of the force with which such an illustration would speak to one familiar with the Roman practice; how it would serve to impress upon him the assurance that the adopted son of God becomes, in a peculiar and intimate sense, one with the heavenly Father ("Conversion of the Roman Empire").'"[(a)]

[(a)] Vincent, Marvin. Ibid. Vol. IV. 91.

[250] "Further examples include: Mt 8:11-12, 'sons of the reign / kingdom,' as in our present verse. Mt 9:15, 'sons of the bridechamber,' means the friends of the bride or groom; members of the wedding party. Mt 23:15, 'sons of *Gehenna*,' means those that will end up in the waste pile, or the dump (note: *Gehenna* was the dump outside Jerusalem). Mk 3:17, Boanerges, 'sons of thunder,' means loud and explosive, impetuous, bold, daring. Lk 10:6, 'son of peace,' means a person whose nature is peace.

Lk 16:8, 'sons of this age ... sons of light,' means those having the character of the one, or the other. Jn 12:36, 'sons of light,' which came from believing into the Light. Ac 4:36, Barnabas, 'son of consolation,' refers to his character. Acts 13:10, Elymas the sorcerer, Paul called him a 'son of the devil,' which he went on to explain as 'an enemy of righteousness.' Ps 89:22, 'son of wickedness,' means a person who does wicked things. Dt 13:13, 'sons of Belial,' means people who live in a worthless manner." — Jonathan Mitchell, author of TNT. Email correspondence from Jonathan Mitchell.

[251] See Jn 8:41, 44.

[252] See also: 1Jn ch 3; also 4:7-11, 20-21.

[253] Mt 13:34b

[254] Mt 16:18, 23

[255] For example: Ez 4:22,23; Dt 1:31; 8:5; 14:1; Ps 103:13; Jer 3:22; 31:20; Hos 11:1-4; Mal 3:17. Robert H. Stein, contributor for *Baker's Evangelical Dictionary.* wrote: "This metaphor for God [Father] may have been avoided in the Old Testament due to its frequent use in the ancient Near East where it was used in various fertility religions and carried heavy sexual overtones."[a]

[a] Stein, Robert H. *Baker's Evangelical Dictionary*. www.biblestudytools.com. Grand Rapids: Baker Pub Group, 1996.

[256] Apparently, in the sense of being compared with a perfect, Holy God.

[257] "Fervently." See Amplified Bible, "footnote: a. G. Abbott-Smith, *Manual Greek Lexicon.*"

[258] Lk 15:11-32

[259] cf. Heb 12:5-11.
Barclay, William. *The Letter to the Hebrews.* Revised Edition. The Daily Study Bible Series. Philadelphia: Westminster Press, 1976. 179.

[260] 1Jn 4:8, 16

[261] Jesus had no problem comparing God as our Father with us as parents. (Mt 7:11)

[262] See Anchor 8.

[263] Heb 12:5-11

[264] Professor Terry L. Miethe, Dean of the Oxford Study Center, G.Brit, and Managing Editor of Moody Press wrote, "The Bible says Christ takes away the sin of the world and is the Savior of the world. A study of the word 'world'— especially in John where it is used 78 times—shows that the world is God-hating, Christ-rejecting, and Satan-dominated. Elwell ... said: 'Yet that is the world for which Christ died. There is not one place in the entire New Testament where "world" means "church" or "the elect."'[a] For more evidence of God's universal love, see article: *The Universality of God's Love* by Dr. Fritz Guy (theology professor), La Sierra University, Riverside, CA.

[a] Pinnock, Clark, ed. *The Grace of God and the Will of Man.* Minneapolis: Bethany House, 1989. 80.

[265] Rom 5:6, 8, 10; 1Pt 3:18

[266] See Question #5. Christ died for people, not things. (Heb 2:9; 1Jn 2:2)

[267] Allin, Thomas. Ibid. 76-77.

[268] Jn 10:30; 14:9; 10:38

[269] The context is Jesus' *death for all* (v. 15)—meaning the cross. Paul specified (v. 18) that God has reconciled us *through Jesus Christ,* which happened, on the cross. Paul concludes by saying God made Jesus to *be sin for us* (v. 21), again—on the cross. It's *all* the cross. Paul *determined* to know nothing except Jesus Christ *and Him crucified.* (1Cor 2:2) The cross is at the core of Paul's theology and this passage.

[270] If God is truly Love (1Jn 4:8, 16) and love is defined as "dying for another" (1Jn 3:16), then it is reasonable to believe that the Father also suffered with His Son, since the Father loves His Son and they are one. (Jn 10:30) The fact that the Father is "greater" than the Son (Jn 14:28) reinforces my conviction. For if the Father didn't suffer (share in the pains of the Son in a personal way), He would be "lesser."

[271] Mt 1:23 quoted from Is 7:14.

[272] 1Cor 13:8 RSV. "Never ends" is stated in one form or another in the following 20 translations: RSV, NRSV, ERV, ESV, EXB, GW, GNT, PME, LEB, TLB, MOUNCE, NOG, NCV, NET, NLV, WE, LB, TEV, JB, NEB.

[273] See www.HopeForAllFellowship.com/GodsLove

[274] 1Pt 3:10-11; Acts 10:34-35; 17:30-31

[275] "Is anything too hard for the Lord?" (Gn 18:14) "There is *nothing* too hard for You." (Jer 32:17) "I am ... the God of all flesh. Is there anything too hard for me?" (Jer 32:27) "Who then can be saved? ... With humans this is impossible, but with God all things are possible." (Mt 19:25-26) Jesus said, "Abba Father, all things are possible for you." (Mk 14:36) The angel said, "with God nothing will be impossible." (Lk 1:35-37) "Who then can be saved?" Jesus replied, "The things which are impossible with humans are possible with God." (Lk 18:26-27)

[276] Acts 9:1-22

[277] Acts 9:15

[278] 1Tm 1:15

[279] EXB, NCV, NET, ICB

[280] "[Jesus] gave Himself a ransom for all, to be testified in due time." (1Tm 2:6)

[281] Rom 2:11; 10:12; Gal 2:6; Eph 6:9; Col 3:25; 1Tm 2:3-4; Jas 3:17; 1Pt 1:17; Ps 145:9

[282] Eph 2:7. www.HopeForAllFellowship.com/Ruling

[283] Even if, initially, it is with a "feigned" submission or with "cringing," as expressed in other translations, "The fear of the Lord is the *beginning* of wisdom." (Prv 9:10) But "perfect love casts out fear." (1Jn 4:18) Read Ps 66:3-4 as one thought: "How awesome

are Your works! Through the greatness of Your power Your enemies shall submit themselves to You. All the earth shall worship You and sing praises to You." Note how verse 4 confirms the accuracy of verse 3 in the NKJV.

[284] Shinn, Quillen Hamilton. *Good Tidings.* Boston: UPH, 1900. p. 81. E-book can be read free here: www.openlibrary.org

[285] Hurley, Loyal F. *The Outcome of Infinite Grace.* Santa Clarita, CA: Concordant Publishing Concern, 1960. 40-41.

[286] Talbott, Thomas. *The Inescapable Love of God.* 2nd Ed. Eugene: Wipf and Stock, 2014. Ch 11, loc 3817.

[287] See www.HopeForAllFellowship.com/FreeWill

[288] Lk 1:37. See note 275 for quotations.

[289] See also Phil 1:6; 2:13; 3:21; 4:13; Eph 2:10; Jn 15:5; Mi 7:19.

[290] Let's follow the example of Abraham: "He did *not waver* at the promise of God through unbelief, but was strengthened in faith, giving *glory* to God, and being *fully convinced* that what He had promised He was also *able* to perform. And therefore it was accounted to him for righteousness.'" (Rom 4:20-21)

[291] See Rom 7:18-19; 23-25.

[292] Even in *Hades,* God and the Lamb (Jesus) are with us! "If I should go down into *Hades*, you are at hand." (Ps 139:8 ABP) "If I make my bed in *Sheol* [G *Hades*] behold, you are there." (Ps 139:8 NAS) Even in the "lake of fire," we are in the "presence" of the Lamb! (Rv 14:10)

[293] Ez 36:25-27; Mi 7:19; Acts 3:25-26; Eph 2:10; Phil 2:13. What God does for Israel He will do for all—see Anchor 9, Promise 3 (Rom 11:26) and Anchor 8.

[294] "Being confident of this very thing, that He who has begun a good work in you *will complete it.* ... " (Phil 1:6)

[295] Is 53:6; Rom 3:23; Jas 2:10; 1Jn 3:4

[296] Rom 4:15; Gal 6:7; Col 3:25. See Anchor 3.

[297] Galatians 3:17

[298] Think of God's commands not so much as things we must do (which we should), but instead, as prophetic declarations of what we will certainly do once God becomes "*all in all*" of us. (1Cor 15:28) For example: "You *shall* [will certainly] not commit adultery. ... You *shall* [will certainly] not steal. ... You *shall* [will certainly] not covet, etc. Doesn't that change everything? See Anchor 8, "Unlimited Power of God's Love." See Peter Hiett's inspiring video confirming our Father's infinite love and power in fulfilling His promises for all humanity: www.youtube.com/watch?v=NO9_SMbLpt8

[299] Strong, James. Ibid. 29. G1670

[300] Jn 18:10; Jn 21:11; Acts 16:19 NAS; Acts 21:30 NAS; Jas 2:6

[301] Rom 5:18 Note "r": "From the context, one can tell what he is saying: that just as one transgression (or the transgression of one man) brought condemnation to all human beings, so by one rectifying act (or the rectifying act of one man) all human beings receive a rectification of life (meaning either a rectification of their lives or a retification imparted by the life of the risen Christ. ... The strict proportionality of the formulation, however, is quite clear, here and in the surrounding verses: just as the first sin brought condemnation and death to *absolutely everyone*, so Christ's act of righteousness brings righteousness and life to *absolutely everyone*. Whether intentional or not, the plain meaning of the verse is that of universal condemnation annulled by universal salvation."

Rom 5:19 Note "s": "The use of the definite article here and elsewhere must be scrupulously observed, in keeping with the traditional way of formulating the distinction between the unique singular and the comprehensive plural in Greek (which a language without articles, like Latin, cannot reflect): not, that is, "one" (in the sense of "someone") and "many" (in the sense of a mere plurality of "someones"), but "the one" (in the sense of the unique and irreplaceable, an irreducible singular) and "the many" (in the sense of all and everyone, the indivisible totality of all particulars). As in the prior verse, the proportion uniting both halves of the formulation is that of the particular and the universal, both in sin and in salvation."[a]

[a] Hart, David Bentley. *The New Testament: A Translation.* New Haven: Yale University Press, 2017. 297-298. Footnotes "r" and "s."

[302] 1Cor 15:45

[303] Note the reaction Paul anticipated: "Shall we continue in sin that grace may abound?" (Rom 6:1) This is similar to a common question that comes up: "Why not sin as we please if God forgives everyone in the end?" That is very revealing. If the Gospel we share with others does not lead them to respond like this, we are not preaching as Paul preached.

[304] See also: Is 45:25; Jer 31:33-34; 32:40; Ez 36:26-27; Rom 11:1-2; Heb 8:10-11.

[305] "I will make you [Abram] a great nation. ... You shall *be* a blessing. ... And in you *all* the families of the earth shall be blessed." (Gn 12:2-3) Though Israel failed in the past, as we all have, God's purposes will yet be realized through Israel in the fullness of time.

[306] Paul writes, "The privilege is great from every point of view. First of all, because the Jews were entrusted with God's truth." (Rom 3:2 WEY)

[307] Rom 2:11. Also Nm 16:22; Ps 145:9; Acts 10:34; Gal 2:6; Eph 6:9; Col 3:25; 1Tm 2:3-4; 1Pt 1:17

[308] Acts 15:8-9. See also Rom 10:12-13; Eph 2:11-18; 3:6. We are all heirs with Israel and thus share in their salvation.

[309] "To you [Jews] *first*, God, having raised up his servant Jesus, sent Him to bless you, in turning away *every one* of you from your iniquities." (Acts 3:26)

[310] Moses and Jeremiah referred to Israel as God's "firstfruit," not His only fruit. (Ex 4:22; Jer 2:3)

[311] Dodd, C. H. *The Epistle to the Romans.* The Moffat New Testament Commentary. Harper and Brother Pub, 1932. 183.
From Mitchell, Jonathan. *Just Paul: Comments on Romans.* Harper Brown Pub. 2014 (Rom 11:32).

[312] *zōopoieō* G2227 is the verb form of *zōē* G2222, and refers to something positive. W. E. Vine defines it as, "to make alive, cause to live, quicken" from *zōē*, "life," and *poieō*, "to make." *Zōē* is the same word used in John 3:16 and in more than 130 New Testament passages. "I am the way, the truth, and the life [*zōē*]." (Jn 14:6) It is used 12 times: Jn 5:21a, 21b; 6:63; Rom 4:17; 8:11; 1Cor 15:22, 36, 45; 2Cor 3:6; Gal 3:21; 1Tm 6:13; 1Pt 3:18. If you will look at each of them, you will see that annihilation or everlasting torment makes no sense in any of them.

[313] See www.HopeForAllFellowship.com/EveryKnee

[314] See Question #5. Christ died for people, not things. (Heb 2:9; 1Jn 2:2)

[315] Jesus is the author and finisher of our faith. (Heb 12:2; also Lk 22:32) We are God's workmanship. (Eph 2:8-10)

[316] See Question #5. Christ died for people, not things. (Heb 2:9; 1Jn 2:2)

[317] Jesus died for the ungodly, sinners, enemies and unjust! (Rom 5:6, 8, 10; 1Pt 3:18)

[318] "Lamb ... slain from the foundation of the world." (Rv 13:8) See also Anchor 1, "Before Time Began."

[319] "Who doth will all men to be saved." (MYLT)

[320] Vine, W. E. Ibid. Section II, 162. G2309.

[321] "Especially" (*malista* G3122) occurs 11 times in the New Testament. In none of them do they mean "exclusively." "Especially" and "exclusively" are different concepts—they are not interchangeable. Review the 11 passages, and you will see that "especially" does not exclude anyone: Acts 20:38; 25:26; 26:2-3; Gal 6:9-10; Phil 4:20-23; 1Tm 5:3-8; 5:16-18; 2Tm 4:13; Ti 1:10-11; Phil 16; 2Pt 2:9-11.

[322] All will know we are His disciples—if we love one another. (Jn 13:35)

[323] " ... in due time" as we saw in the previous passage (1Tm 2:6).

[324] "For *all* have sinned." (Rom 3:23)

[325] www.HopeForAllFellowship.com/Promises

[326] Gal 3:17

[327] "Because of the hope which is laid up for you in heaven ... the gospel ... is bringing forth fruit .... since the day you heard and knew the grace of God in truth." (Col 1:5-6)

[328] www.youtube.com/watch?v=NO9_SMbLpt8 "I Should You Not" by Peter Hiett, from the "Downside Up Series" extols our Father's infinite love and power in fulfilling His promises for all people.

[329] Aiken, Mercy. "If Hell Is Real."
www.tentmaker.org/articles/ifhellisrealprintable.htm/

[330] See Question #5. Christ died for people, not things. (Heb 2:9; 1Jn 2:2)

[331] Ramelli, Ilaria Ph.D. *The Christian Doctrine of Apokatastasis: A Critical Assessment from the New Testament to Eriugena (Supplements to Vigiliae Christianae).* n.p.:BRILL, 2013. Also see Anchor 1, "The Early Church."

[332] Mt 11:15 NIV; 13:9, 43; Mt 4:9; 4:23; 7:16; Lk 8:8; Rv 2:7, 11, 17, 29; 3:6, 13, 22.

[333] See: www.HopeForAllFellowship.com/Sodom. See Ez 16:53-55; 36:19-36, 38; especially: Is 19:22-25.

[334] Lk 24:25, 27, 31-32

[335] Acts 10:36 and 20:24 NIV; Rom 10:15; Lk 2:10

[336] "The fruit of the Spirit is love, *joy, peace*. ... " (Gal 5:20) The Kingdom of God is righteousness, *peace* and *joy*. ... " (Rom 14:17) In the context of salvation (v. 5) Peter said we *greatly rejoice* (v. 6), and "you *rejoice* with *joy inexpressible* and full of glory." (1Pt 1:8) Paul said, "May the God of hope fill you with *all joy* and *peace* in believing." (Rom 15:13)

[337] "Isaiah alluded to this unique event when he predicted the work of the future Messiah. (Is 61:1-3, 11) And, Jesus, when He returned from being tempted by the devil, went into the synagogue in Nazareth and read from that specific passage in Isaiah to announce His purpose for coming–' ... to proclaim freedom for the prisoners and recovery of sight for the blind, to release the oppressed, to proclaim the year of the Lord's favor'—Lk 4:18-21. Jesus came to release *all* from bondage to sin and death. The great Jubilee Festival foreshadowed what He would ultimately do."[a]

[a] Sarris, George W. *Heaven's Doors: Wider Than You Ever Believed!* Trumbull: GWS Publishing, 2017. 211-212.

[338] Rom 8:19-22; 1Cor 15:22-28; Phil 2:9-11

[339] God's "chosen" or "elect" are His firstfruits, not His only fruit; c.f. Acts 3:25-26; Jas 1:18; Rv 14:4.

[340] See Anchor 9, Promise 6.

[341] Jesus quotes Isaiah (61:1-3) who lived c. 740-681 BC.
www.thenagain.info/WebChron/WestCiv/Isaiah.html

[342] Lk 6:20-21 (part of what is known as "The Beatitudes")

[343] Since Jesus comforts all who mourn (which must be fullfilled in the coming ages, since not everyone is comforted now), endless punishment cannot be true. Who could *ever* be comforted if they feared that they or a loved one might suffer forever?

[344] For example, according to her attorney, Andrea Yates drowned her five small children to "save" them. She believed her children "needed to die in order to be saved" because she believed "she was such a bad mother that she was causing them to

deteriorate and be doomed to the fires of eternal damnation."[a]

[a] Sweetingham, Lisa. "Defense: Yates Killed Kids to Save Them." *CNN.com*. 27 June 2006. www.cnn.com/2006/LAW/06/26/yates.trial/index.html

[345] Nyland, Dr. A. Ibid. 490.

[346] Barclay, William. *The Revelation of John*. Vol. 1. Revised Ed. The Daily Bible Study Series. Philadelphia: Westminster Press, 1976. 20.

[347] Revelation: 94-96 AD; Matthew's Gospel: 50-60 AD.

MacArthur, John. "When Were the Bible Books Written?" *Grace To You*. QA176. www.gty.org.

[348] Vincent, Marvin. Ibid. Vol. III. 389.

Vincent defines "the lower parts of the earth" as "the under world." The reference is to Christ's descent into *Hades*.

[349] NKJV footnote: NU-Text and M-Text read "nations" (as in most modern versions).

[350] This prophetic statement fits the context of the closing chapters of Revelation because it: 1. Refers to the future state of Jerusalem. 2. Includes "all" nations. 3. Speaks of the transformation of the human heart. I cannot imagine another era that better applies to this terminology, especially in light of the "all" promises listed in Anchor 9.

[351] See also: Rv 16:14; 17:2; 18:3, 9; Acts 4:26.

[352] The majority of modern translations, based on the earliest manuscripts, read similar to the NAS and NIV.

[353] Thomas Talbott writes, "Concerning 'the kings of the earth' and other incoming traffic into the new Jerusalem, [Vernard] Eller writes: 'Both of these—"the kings of the earth" and "the wealth and splendor of the nations"—are terms John has used often enough, consistently enough, and with enough pointed overtone, that it simply is inconceivable that he could have written them this time offhandedly, carelessly, without thinking of what he was doing. ... In that lake of fire something has happened to these kings that makes them entirely different people, gives them an entirely different significance than they had before.'"[a]

See Eller's *The Most Revealing Book in the Bible*. Grand Rapids: Eerdmans Publishing Company, 1974. 200-201.

[a] Talbott, Thomas. Ibid. Section: "Two Very Different Images: The Lake of Fire and the Outer Darkness." p. 3 footnote.

[354] NIV, NAS, etc. or "obey His commands" (KJV, NKJV)—it depends on which Greek text your Bible is based on. I believe they are interchangeable—two sides of one truth. Rv 19:8 says, "fine linen is the righteous acts of the saints." In any case, our "righteous acts" come from God's power working in us (Eph 2:8-10; Phil 2:13).

[355] 1Jn 1:7. Prof. Talbott authorized me to insert the words in brackets for clarification.

[356] Talbott, Thomas. Ibid.

See also *The Evangelical Universalist* by Gregory MacDonald, 2nd Ed. 114-120.

[357] Priests serve as ambassadors, proclaim the Gospel, reign with Christ, pray and intercede for the lost and the saints. (2Cor 5:20; Mt 9:38; 19:28; Lk 19:17-19; 1Tm 2:1; 2Tm 2:12; Rv 1:6; 5:10; 22:3, 5)

[358] See Anchor 4, "Greek *Eis tous aiōnas tōn aiōnōn*" for the meaning of this phrase.

[359] God's servants are the Good Shepherd's eyes, hands and feet, searching for His lost sheep *until* He finds them. They manifest His compassionate heart for a world of lost people. (Jn10:11; Mt 9:36-38) Surely He is not less caring of His sheep than He expects us to be for ours. (Lk 15:4, 7)

[360] This purpose remains unchanged; Christ is the same yesterday, today and forever. (Heb 13:8) The Gospel will always be proclaimed as long as there are lost people in need of Jesus. "And I saw another messenger flying in mid-heaven, having good news age-during [*aiōnios* G166—encompasses all ages] to proclaim to those dwelling upon the earth, and to every nation, and tribe, and tongue, and people." (Rv 14:6 YLT)

[361] Review point 6 above.

[362] They can enter, since they are no longer defiled. (Rv 21:27)

[363] The TNT reads: "to the end that within the continuously oncoming ages He may exhibit (display; point out; give proof of)." See: CJB; DARBY; HCSB; ISV; AMP; DLNT; GNT; MOUNCE; NET.

[364] "When [his son] was still a great way off, his father saw him and had compassion, and ran and fell on his neck and kissed him [fervently[a]]." (Lk 15:20)

[a] AMP footnote: G. Abbott-Smith, *Manual Greek Lexicon*.

[365] See Question #26.

[366] Heb 12:29

[367] William Barclay says: "The Bride, we know, is the Church."[a]

[a] Barclay, William. Ibid. 229.

[368] 2Pt 3:15

[369] Mt 1:21; Heb 2:9; Jn 3:17; 12:47; 17:4

[370] Phil 2:9-11. See also Is 45:23; Rom 14:11; 1Cor 15:22-28; Heb 12:5; 2:8-9.

[371] A "new name," like other Biblical concepts, may have several connotations. It may refer to over-comers destined to reign with Christ in an age to come (2Tim 2:12; Rv 2:17) or to a title of an office in His government. (Lk 19:16-17) Another connotation, in light of God's nature and promises (Anchors 8 and 9), is that a new name is our destiny. "If anyone is in Christ, he is a *new* creation; old things have passed away ... all things [names included] become *new*." (2Cor 5:17) A new name signifies a change of identity. Abram became Abraham—"father of a multitude," Sarai became Sarah—"princess," Jacob became Israel—"prince of God," Simon became Peter—the "rock" and Saul became Paul—Christ' chosen vessel to the Nations. (Acts 9:15)

[372] Mal 3:6; Jas 1:17

[373] "Consider this! I am presently making all things new (or: habitually creating everything [to be] new and fresh; progressively forming [the] whole anew; or, reading the Greek *panta* as masculine: periodically making *all humanity* new; progressively creating *every person* anew; constantly constructing [as corporate being] *all people* fresh and new; continuously renewing *everyone*)!" (Rv 21:5 TNT)

[374] NIV: "the gates of Hades will not overcome it [or prove stronger than it—NIV fn]." JB: "the gates of the underworld can never hold out against it [the gates symbolize the power of the underworld to hold captives—JB fn]."

[375] 1Pt 3:19-4:6. See Anchor 5, "Hope in Death," numbers 14-16.

[376] Rv 1:17-18

[377] "You are Peter, and on this rock I will build my church and the gates of *Hades* shall not prevail against it. And *I will give you the keys* of the kingdom ... whatever you bind [and loose] on earth will be bound in heaven." (Mt 16:18-19) Peter merely represents all who reign with Christ. "You have made us [God's worshipers] kings and priests to our God; and we shall reign on the earth." (Rv 5:10)

[378] Lk 4:18; Is 61:1

[379] Eph 4:8; Ps 68:18

[380] In Col. 1:25, Paul says he became a minister to make the word of God fully known (RSV) or to complete the word of God. (Darby, CLT) See also Acts 9:15; Rom 11:13. See www.HopeForAllFellowship.com/LastThings

[381] "He" [Christ] who is excepted in verse 27, subjects Himself in verse 28. This affirms that the phrase "all things," refers to "all persons." See Question #5.

[382] NAS

[383] RSV, CEV, AMPC

[384] *Hypotassō*, G5293. www.blueletterbible.org/nasb/1co/15/1/t_conc_1077027

[385] They being ignorant of God's righteousness ... have not submitted [G5293] to the righteousness of God ... righteousness to everyone who believes." (Rom 10:3-4)

[386] Hebrews 2:8-10 confirms this. "You have put all things in subjection under his feet. For in that He put all in subjection under him, *He left nothing that is not put under him. But now we do not yet see* all things put under him. *But we see Jesus* ... [who] might taste death for *everyone."* The beauty here is that God's amazing promise for all, though not yet evident ("we do not *yet* see," v. 8b) will surely be fulfilled as the word "yet" implies. All will subject themselves (in God's time) to Jesus, who tasted death for everyone (v. 9b).

[387] 1Cor 15:28

[388] Jn 4:42; 1Jn 4:14

[389] "Every creature ... in heaven and on the earth and under the earth ... and all that are in them, I heard saying: 'Blessing and honor and glory and power be to Him who sits

on the throne!'" (Rv 5:13) Note that verses 3-4 affirm the presence of all humanity in this most glorious event.

[390] CEB, MSG, NIRV, TLV

[391] Jn 16:12-13 Note: How long this will take is not defined. The Church is still very divided. We have not yet come into the unity Jesus prayed for in John 17.

[392] For at least a thousand years before Martin Luther launched the reformation revolution in 1517, the Church was ruled by popes and the Scriptures were not available in the languages of the world. But Gutenberg's printing press was now available. For the first time in history, mass printing enabled Luther to bring his message directly to the people.[a]

[a] Kramer, Patrick. "Martin Luther and the Printing Press." *Infoage*. 29 Sept 2011. www.patrickkramer.umwblogs.org/2011/09/29/martin-luther-and-the-printing-press/.

[393] See *Martin Luther: The Man Who Rediscovered God and Changed the World* by Eric Metaxas. Amazon.

[394] "But, beloved, do not forget this one thing, that with the Lord one day is as a thousand years, and a thousand years as one day." (2 Pt 3:8)

[395] 1 Cor 13:9-12

[396] This Catholic priest, from humble beginnings, went on to the highest post in his church—named Person of the Year by Time magazine in 2013. "He has embarked on a tenure characterized by humility and outspoken support of the world's poor."[a]

[a] https://www.biography.com/people/pope-francis-21152349

[397(a)] Homily at Chapel of Domus Sanctae Marthae, 22 May, 2013. In context: www.HopeForAllFellowship.com/Homily [a] Glatz, Carol. "Vatican statistics: Church growth remains steady worldwide." Catholic Herald. 5 May 2014.

[398] Is 2:2 (NIV)

[399] Have you noticed the words of the songs Christ's followers are singing in our generation—how more and more they extol God's great love for all people? Have we been listening? The Holy Spirit in our younger generation is revealing a higher view of God and His purposes for all humanity. Listen to their anointed lyrics—often a step ahead of our clergy.

[400] The Introduction to *The [expanded] Bible*^{TM} states, "No translation is ever completely successful, however, whether of the Bible or any other text. All translations fall short for a variety of reasons. First, no two languages are equivalent in their vocabulary, sounds, rhythms, idioms, or underlying structure. Nor are any two cultures out of which languages arise equivalent in their way of understanding and expressing reality, their value systems, or their social and political organization, among other factors. Second, the meaning of a text includes much more than its abstract thought. The sounds and rhythms of words, word play and puns, emotional overtones, metaphor, figurative language, and tone are just some of the other devices that carry meaning. No translation can transfer all these things from one language to another. Third, all translations require interpretation. One cannot convey meaning in a second language without first deciding what it means in the original. This step of interpretation in translation is unavoidable

and imperfect; equally skilled and well-meaning scholars will interpret differently. Fourth, a traditional translation requires one to choose a single possibility—whether of a word or an interpretation—when in fact two or more may be plausible."[a]

[a] Longman, Tremper III, Mark L. Strauss and Daniel Taylor. Version Information. "An Introduction to the [expanded] Bible™." *The Expanded Bible. Bible Gateway.* Thomas Nelson, 2011. www.biblegateway.com.

[401] Also, translators must follow the guidelines established by the entities funding their work, who cater to the established religious traditions. For example, the KJV translators were mandated by the king to not compromise the doctrines of the Church. See their official translation guidelines numbers 1 and 4.

[a] Hall, Isaac H., ed. Ibid. www.bible-researcher.com/kjvhist.html

[402] "When He, the Spirit of truth, has come, He will guide you into all truth." (Jn 16:13) See also Lk 24:32, 45; 8:10; Jn 8:43, 47; Mt 6:23; 13:9-11, 16; 15:6.

[403] Lk 12:57; 1Thes 5:21

[404] No one has perfect knowledge about God and the Bible's teachings. No commandment says, "You must not hold any mistaken beliefs or else. ... " See the Ten Commandments, for example. (Ex 20:1-17) Guilt and judgment are based on our knowledge of what sin is. James said, "To him who knows to do good and does not do it, to him it is sin." (Jas 4:17) Paul says: "I was once alive [not held accountable] ... when I did not know what the Law said I had to do. Then I found that I had broken the Law, ... [and I died (NKJV) i.e., held accountable with its consequences from then on]." (Rom 7:9 NLV) See also Lk 12:47-48.

[405] Paul writes, "I persecuted this Way [Christians] to the death, binding and delivering into prisons both men and women, as also the high priest bears me witness, and all the council of the elders, from whom I also received letters to the brethren, and went to Damascus to bring in chains even those who were there to Jerusalem to be punished." (Acts 22:4-5)

[406] Hopefully, this book will encourage and guide you in searching the Scriptures more deeply and help you appreciate the complexity of the Bible and the need to explore the various possibilities in interpretation. But in addition to all the Bible translations and study aids you might find, the most important thing is hearing from the living Word of God Himself—Jesus. He said, "You search the Scriptures, for in them you think you have eternal life; and these are they which testify of Me. But you are not willing to come to Me that you may have life." (Jn 5:39-40)

The living speaking "Word of God," who transcends all language, time, cultures and any other barriers to truth, is Jesus Himself, as declared plainly in Jn 1:1 and 14. He is the true light which enlightens every person coming into the world. (Jn 1:9) The truth of Scripture must be confirmed by the Spirit of Christ in us for it to be implanted in our minds and to transform our hearts. He said, "The anointing which you have received from Him abides in you, and you do not need that anyone teach you." (1Jn 2:27) "When He, the Spirit of truth, has come, He will guide you into all truth." (Jn 16:13) It is Christ who opens the Scriptures to our understanding (Lk 24: 27, 31-32, 45) and causes our hearts to burn within us (v. 32). *I emphasize* our need of *total dependency* on God, especially in this critical topic of judgment and ultimate human destiny.

[407] We must interpret individual passages in the larger context of what is being said in order to understand what was in the minds of those present at the time. That is partly why I started this book with Anchor 1—History Testifies. We must discern to whom a particular warning is referring to. They are not all meant for us today, or for all of us at the same time. The most severe were addressed to the self-righteous, proud and selfish such as the Pharisees and Sadducees, to whom Jesus urged to flee the coming wrath by producing the fruits of repentance. (Mt 3:7-8) See the seven woes of Mt 23. But to the hurting and humble, only gentle, comforting words were given. Consider the repentant sinner praying in the Temple (Lk 18:9-14) and the woman caught in adultery (Jn 8:6-8). Heath Bradley states: "God comforts the afflicted ... but afflicts the [selfishly] comfortable."[a]

[a] Bradley, Heath. Ibid. 82.

[408] This can occur in the context of the whole Bible (Anchor 1) or the New Testament, not merely in a particular sentence, paragraph, chapter or book, as many assume. This is especially critical when considering such a grave subject as ultimate human destiny. That is why I present ten Anchors of Hope as founding pillars and not merely isolated passages and ideas.

[409] Ancient eastern language abounds in extreme and exaggerated metaphorical language. Anchor 2.

[410] Judgment always has a good purpose even when it is not obvious. Anchor 3.

[411] See Anchors 4 and 5.

[412] See Anchors 3 and 6.

[413] See Anchor 6, "The Unwritten Law—Conscience."

[414] If our view of God is accurate, we will be full of light—if not, darkness. (Mt 6:22-23) Anchor 1, "The Lamp of the Body" and Anchor 6: "The Unwritten Law—Conscience."

[415] Unless Christ opens our minds to the Scriptures, we will remain in the dark. And to whom does He open them? The humble with a teachable spirit: "God has heard your prayers ever since the first day you decided to humble yourself in order to gain understanding. I have come in answer to your prayer." (Dn 10:12 GNT) In the context of a judgment warning (v. 24), Jesus said: "I praise you, Father ... because you have hidden these things from the wise and learned, and revealed them to little children." (Mt 11:24-25 NIV) Beware of those who teach with dogmatic certainty on God's judgments. Be teachable; look deeper for satisfying answers; admit that you're perplexed or confused, lacking understanding. God will honor that. See Lk 24:27, 31-32; Mt 7:7-11; Jn 8:43; 16:13; 2Tm 2:15.

[416] "How unsearchable are His judgments and His ways past finding out!" (Rom 11:33) "For we know in part." (1Cor 13:9) God has not revealed all the details about His

judgments and ways, but He has revealed His Father-heart—His loving character in them. That is the most important thing of all!

[417] See Anchor 9, last paragraph.

[418] 1Cor 13:9-12; Rom 11:33; Mt 11:24-26—context is judgment (v. 24).

[419] Col 1:19-20

[420] See Question 5 and Note 438 to see why "All things" certainly includes people.

[421] Col 1:19-20

[422] "God demonstrates His own love toward us, in that while we were yet sinners, Christ died for us ... reconciled [us] to God through the death of His Son." (Rom 5:8,10)

[423] "We have redemption through His blood, the forgiveness of sins." (Col 1:14)

[424] "If we confess our sins [a relational act], He is faithful and just to forgive us." (1Jn 1:9) Though He forgives, He often lets the consequences of our actions teach us important lessons—which develop our character.

[425] This is vital to harmonizing the Scriptures relative to God's grace in light of His numerous warnings. See Anchor 3, "Synergy of Judgment with Mercy." Also Anchor 6. For more details: www.HopeForAllFellowship.com/Salvation

[426] 2 Cor 5:14.

[427] Jesus suffered "that through death He might ... release those who through fear of death were all their lifetime subject to bondage." (Heb 2:14-15)

[428] Mt 9:36-38 (NAS). He then asked His disciples to pray that God send His servants into the vast world of suffering humanity. How can we not respond to this if we care for humanity like Jesus does?

[429] Rom 10:15. *And* Jesus said, "The Spirit of the Lord is upon Me, because He has anointed Me to preach the gospel to the poor ... sent Me to heal the brokenhearted, to proclaim liberty to the captives and recovery of sight to the blind, to set at liberty those who are oppressed." He quoted from Is 61:1-2 which adds: "to comfort *all* who mourn." (Lk 4:18; 61:2)

[430] Mt 5:14-16; 28:18-20; Lk 10:16a; Mk 16:15; Jn 17:23. And note: there are consequences to how we live our lives as discussed in Anchor 6. That is part of the Gospel, too, and it applies to all.

[431] Jesus' yoke is easy, His burden is light and His commandments are not burdensome (Mt 11:30; 1Jn 5:3) *because* ... He empowers us in love. (Eph 2:10;Phil 1:6, 2:13, 4:13, etc.) Salvation is ultimately becoming like Christ—His values and priorities becoming ours. We no longer live for ourselves but for Him who gave His all for us. Just think what this world could be like if every person on earth walked closely with Jesus Christ. Jesus taught us to pray: "Your Kingdom come, Your will be done on earth as it is in Heaven." (Mt 6:10) This cannot happen without the Gospel.

[432]"By this all will know that you are My disciples, if you have love for one another." (Jn 13:35) "Let your light so shine before men, that they may see your good works and glorify your Father in heaven. (Mt 5:16)

[433] Paul then explains (Col 1: 22) that reconciliation's purpose is to present us holy and blameless and irreproachable in His sight. Our hope in these good tidings plays a key role in empowering our life in Christ. "We love Him because He first loved us." (1Jn 4:19)—not from fear but out of a joyful heart.

[434] See www.HopeForAllFellowship.com/Salvation

[435] DeRose is a Yale philosophy professor, specializing in language.

[436] DeRose, Keith. "Section 3: All." *Universalism and the Bible: The Really Good News. Yale Campus Press.* www.campuspress.yale.edu/keithderose/1129-2/#3

[437] Jesus died for the ungodly, sinners, enemies and unjust! (Rom 5:6, 8, 10; 1Pt 3:18)

[438] Adding "things" often muddies the water when people are the focal point of redemption. Bible translator, Jonathan Mitchell says "all things" in Acts 3:21, is plural as both a masculine and a neuter—*panton*. It can be rendered "all humans."

The CLT says "all" in both Col 1:19 and Acts 3:21. Paul wrote, "Let no one boast in men. For all things are yours: whether Paul or Apollos or Cephas, or the world." (1Cor 3:21-22) The first three "things" are specific persons and "world" simply means all persons everywhere! In Hebrews: "We do not yet see all things put under Him. But we see Jesus [a person]." (Heb 2:8-9) The word "But" means persons are in view! Paul says "all things" are put under Christ's feet, except God [a person]." (1Cor 15:27) "Except" means persons are in view! "All things" are subjected to Christ—then the Son (a person) is also subjected to God. (1Cor 15:28) "Is also" means persons are in view! "He is able even to subdue all things [*ta panta*] to Himself." (Phil 3:21) Mitchell says, "*Ta panta* in no way excludes humanity; it excludes nothing! (The above Mitchell quotes are from a personal email to the author.)

Paul said, "In ... the fullness of the times He might gather together in one all things. ... Also we have obtained an inheritance. ... Who works all things ... that we ... should be to the praise of His glory." (Eph 1:10-12) "Also we" and "that we" assumes persons are included.

The introduction of the TNT states: "The Greek word *pas* (all) G3956, is both masculine and neuter in some of its forms. With many translations you will only find the neuter rendered, for example with a plural, 'all things.'" The TNT gives renderings of both the neuter and the masculine, when such is the case, translating the masculine as "all people; all humanity; or all mankind." This is the case with Acts 3:21, which is plural as both a masculine and a neuter—*panton*. It can be rendered "all humans." See TNT, 2014 Edition, Introduction page 2.

TNT reads: " ... until the periods ... moving all mankind forward." "All things" is based (in its various forms) on the single Greek word *pas* G3956. The KJV translates it: "all" 748x, "all things" 170x, "every" 117x, "all men" 41x, "whosoever" 31x,

"everyone" 28x, etc.
www.blueletterbible.org/lang/lexicon/lexicon.cfm?Strongs=G3956&t=NKJV)
The range of forms of *pas* are: *panta* (masc. sing., neut. pl.); *pantas* (masc. pl.); *pantes* (masc. pl., neut. pl.); *panti* (masc. sing., neut. sing.); *pantos* (masc. sing., neut. sing.); *panton* (masc. pl., neut. pl.); *pas* (masc. sing.); *pasa, pasais, pasan, pasas, pase, pases* (fem.); *pasi* (masc.pl., neut. pl.); *pason* (fem. pl.).

[439] Rom 5: 6, 8, 10; 1Pt 3:18

[440] Mi 7:19: "He will again have compassion on us and will subdue [conquer—EXB, NCV, NET, ICB] our iniquities. Also Acts 3:26; Rom 11:26; Phil 1:6; 2:13; 3:21; Eph 2:10; 3:20.

[441] The key to understanding that God will transform all sinners in "due time" lies in the mystery of the ages, the purpose of election and judgment, the limited nature of death and destruction and the character of God—His father heart, love, promises, power and determined will to save all people. God's plan for us cannot fail.

[442] *orgē* G3709

[443] See CJB, ERV, EXB, GNT, GW, ICB, JB, LB, NCV, NIRV, NOG, OJB, PME, NLT, NLV, REB , TLB, SNT, WEY, MYLT for example.

[444] Mt 7:1-2; Anchor 6, "The Written Law."

[445] *Oxford American Desk Dictionary and Thesaurus*. Second Ed. New York: Berkley, 2001. 28.

[446] Judgment is always measured—according to deeds: Ps 62:12; Prv 24:12; Is 59:18; Jer 17:10; 25:14; Ez 24:14; 36:19; Hos 12:2; Zec 1:6; Mt 6:14-15; 7:1; 16:27; 18:34-35; Mk 4:24; 11:25-26; Lk 12:47-48, 59; 14:14; 18:14; Rom 2:6; 2Cor 5:10; 11:15; Gal 6:7; Eph 6:8; Col 3:25; 2Tm 4:14; Jas 2:13; 1Pt 1:17; Rv 2:23; 18:6; 20:12-13; 22:12. See Anchor 6, "The Written Law."

[447] Rom 9:15; 11:32. See Anchor 3, "Synergism of Judgment with Mercy."

[448] Romans 12:19-21 says, "My dear friends, do not seek revenge, but [give place to wrath (*orgē*)—NKJV] leave a place for divine retribution [*orgē*]; for there is a text which reads, 'Justice is mine, says the Lord, I will repay.'"(NEB) Scripture interprets itself in this passage. *Orgē* is interchanged with the idea of justice—"I will repay." To "repay" means to recompense what is due—no more, no less. The passage ends with evil being defeated by good. *Orgē* then, should be understood as something positive and purposeful.

In Romans 1:18, it is directed against sin, which affirms the adage: "God loves the sinner but hates the sin." In its "severest form" [WEY] *orgē* comes upon the Jews (1Thes 2:15-16) whom Paul says will *all* be saved. (Rom 11:26) Thus it cannot be endless or merciless! In Revelation 15:1 and 8, the first and last verses, God's wrath comes to completion. What is "completed" is not eternal! Sandwiched between verses one and eight is this amazing promise: "Great and marvelous are Your works, Lord God

Almighty! Just and true are Your ways, O King of the [nations—NAS]! Who shall not fear You, O Lord, and glorify Your name? [Everyone will!] For You alone are holy. For all nations shall come and worship before You, for Your judgments have been manifested." (vs. 3-4)

God's wrath ends with all nations worshiping God! Verse 8 says, "no one was able to enter the temple till the seven plagues [God's wrath] ... were completed." Once wrath is completed, everyone will enter! This must allude to the sinners who wash their robes and enter the Holy City in chapters 21 and 22. —see Anchor 10. "For I will not contend forever, nor will I always be angry; for the spirit would fail before Me, and the souls which I have made." (Is 57:16) See Jer 23:20; 30:24; Is 2:2-4.

The wrath of God that "abides" on us (Jn 3:36) is a present state. The CLT reads: " ... the indignation of God is remaining on him." The TNT reads: "God's personal emotion and inherent fervor is *continuously remaining* upon him." No one, while in unbelief, is "seeing" life, i.e., taking hold of that which is *life indeed* (1Tm 6:19 NAS), or *truly life* (NIV). Jesus called it *abundant life.* (Jn 10:10)

If wrath was a hopeless state, none of us could ever be saved [delivered, rescued, made healthy and whole—TNT], since we were all, at one time, in unbelief. "God hath concluded them all in unbelief, that He might have mercy upon all." (Rom 11:32 KJV) See Anchor 3, "Synergism of Judgment with Mercy."

[449] See: CEV, ERV, EXB, GW, GNT, ICB, ISV, LB, NOG, NCV, NIV, NIRV, NIVUK, NLT, PME, TLB, TEV, VOICE, WE, WYC, TNT. Also Today's New International Version, Worldwide English NT. Wycliff Bible, 2001.

[450] Mt 26:56 KJV

[451] Mk 3:14 KJV

[452] Eph 2:6-7 KJV

[453] Dr. Michael Jones, a Hebrew and Greek scholar, explained to me in an email: "Using 'might' in John 3:17 is not good translating. The force of the subjunctive here "ἵνα σωθῇ" is not like a maybe, or a might. That is why many translators leave 'might' out, i. e., to keep the English-only reader from getting confused. The subjunctive can be a might, i.e., a possibility–a maybe–a might, and yet, it can also emphasize a statement of fact better than the indicative mood/mode."

[454] "Perish" is *apollumi* G622—the same word translated as "lost." We are all born "perishing." We are dead until God makes us alive in Christ. (Eph 2:1) "Let the dead bury their dead." (Mt 8:22) "She who lives in pleasure is dead while she lives." (1Tm 5:6). See Anchor 5, "Hope in Destruction."

[455] NTAT. "Life of the Ages" (WEY). "life eonian" (CTL). "But rather can continuously have eonian life (age-durative life with qualities derived from the Age; life of and for the ages)." (TNT) "life of the world to come." The Nicene Creed. See Anchor 4, "Greek *Aiōnios*."

[456] Jn 17: 3

[457] Jesus declared: "I did not come to judge the world but *to save* the world."(Jn 12:47)

[458] Jn 3:16-17 NIV

[459] Prof. R.V.G. Tasker: "Aiōnios is a qualitative rather than a quantitative word. Eternal life is the life that is characteristic of the age [*aiōn*] to come." Peter Hiett refers to this as "God's age." See Anchor 4.

[460] Joseph Dillow, Th.D. Dallas Theological Seminary, explained, "Salvation is a broad term. It commonly means 'to make whole,' 'to sanctify,' 'to endure victoriously,' or 'to be delivered from some general trouble or difficulty.' Without question, the common 'knee-jerk' reaction which assumes that 'salvation' always has eternal deliverance in view, has seriously compromised the ability of many to objectively discern what the New Testament writers intended to teach."[a]

[a] Dillow, Joseph. *The Reign of the Servant Kings*. Hayesville, NC: Schoettle, 1992. 132-133.

[461] Mt 18:11

[462] 1Tm 1:15; Mt 1:21; Compare Gal 3:8 with Acts 3:25-26 NAS.

[463] See www.HopeForAllFellowship.com/Salvation

[464] NTAT

[465] Jn 17:3; Heb 8:11-12; Review Anchor 8.

[466] Lk 20:38. Review Anchor 5.

[467] The word damnation is not found in the ASV, ESV, GNT, HCSB, PME, NAS, NCV, NET, NKJV, NLV, NLT, NIV, NRSV, RSV, MYLT, etc.

[468] Defined as "a (religious) ban or (concretely) excommunicated (thing or person). Strong, James. Ibid. 6. G331.

[469] *Oxford American Desk Dictionary.* Ibid. 186. First listing and most appropriate to this context.

[470] Rom 9:3; Acts 23:14. Paul wished it on himself to spare his fellow Israelites.

[471] "For I was wishing, I myself, to be *anathema* from the Christ—for my brethren, my kindred, according to the flesh." (Rom 9:3 MYLT). His great love for his fellow Israelites led him to wish he could switch places with them to their benefit. In other words, he would be accepting their righteous, age-abiding judgment for having rejected Christ in this life, knowing that he would ultimately be saved with all Israel as he then states! This is part of a long three-chapter discussion that culminates in all Israel being saved and God's mercy being granted to all (Rom 11:26-32)!

[472] See Anchor 4, "Greek *Aionios.*" Anchor 5, "Hope in Destruction."

[473] With amplication: " … paying the thing that is right (incur justice, fairness and equity): ruin pertaining to the Age [of Messiah] (or: an unspecified period of ruin or

destruction; or: ruin for an age; eonian destruction having the character of the Age; or: life-long ruin).

[474] See Anchors 3, 5 and 6.

[475] The RSV says: "Do justice. ... " TNT: "Continuously giving justice. ..." PME: "Bring full justice. ... " CEB: "Give justice. ... " VOICE: "Deal out perfect justice. ... " Prof. Marvin Vincent says, "Vengeance (KJV) is an unfortunate rendering, as implying, in popular usage, personal vindictiveness. See 2Cor 7:11. It is the full awarding of justice to all parties."[a] He devotes almost four pages (fine print) arguing that the Greek words in this passage do not mean endless penalty.[b]

[a] Vincent, Marvin. Ibid. Vol. 1. 61-62.
[b] Ibid. Vol. 4. 58-62.

[476] SNT. Rom 3:18, footnote 3. Dr. Nyland adds, "See *P.Tebt* I.59, where someone writes to the priests of Tebtunis assuring them of his good will "because from old I revere and worship the temple." The use was the same from Classical times onwards."

[477] The reason people can't see them is because their belief that salvation is only possible *before* death blinds them. They aren't open to it—so they don't notice them, or they assume there's a logical explanation for them. Simply put, they can't connect the dots that support it throughout the Scriptures—"He who has ears to hear, let him hear!" (Mt 11:15)

[478] 1Pt 4:6 (NAS). See Anchor 5, "Hope In Death," points 13-16.

[479] See how translators have changed this text at www.BibleGateway.com.

[480] God made a covenant with Israel through the sure mercies of David—a witness to *the people*, a leader ... "Surely ... *nations* ... shall run to you [Israel] because of the Lord ... Holy One *of Israel;* for He has glorified you [Israel]. Seek the Lord [Israel] while He may be found, call upon Him while He is near." (Is 55:3-6) Israel was called to be God's light to all nations: "Surely ... *nations* ... shall run to you!" (Gn 12:3; 18:18; 22:18; 26:4; 28:14; Acts 3:25-26; Gal 3:8) Note! In spite of all her failings, *all* Israel *will* be saved. (Rom 11:26)

[481] Verse three of Isaiah 55 says: "*Incline your ear,* and *come to Me. Hear,* and your soul shall live [abundantly]." (Is 55:1-3) If we seek Him with all our heart (incline our ear and come to Him), we are able to hear (find) Him; He is not far from any of us. (Dt 4:29; Acts 17:27) But *if* we let our hearts get cold and allow ourselves to drift away from His voice, He will leave us to our own devices *until* we come to the end of ourselves. (Lk 15:17-19) This does *not* mean there's no hope of salvation after death (see Anchor 5). It's about our present relationship with God. Most don't realize that God has already reconciled us all to Himself in Christ. (2Cor 5:19-20; Col 1:21) It is we who need to reconcile ourselves to Him. (2Cor 5:20) He is unchanging! (Mal 3: 6)

[482] His mercies are new every morning. (Lam 3:23) "Now [is] a well-accepted time; lo, now, a day of salvation." (2Cor 6:2 MYLT) The MSG: "Now is the right time to listen, the day to be helped. Don't put it off." Our heavenly Father is always ready to welcome

us home once we realize we're helpless and hopeless apart from Him and desire to return to Him. (Lk 15:20) Don't ever think it's too late to turn to God; He is Love and love never ends. (1Cor 13:8 RSV) It is so tragic that some think these texts imply that our loving Father will at some point no longer extend His mercy and forgiveness to His children. The truth is: "His mercy endures forever!"(Ps 136:1-26)

[483] Mt 10:28-31 (MSG)

[484] Mt 10:31 (NIV)

[485] I base this on the Biblical principles set forth in Anchor 2 ("Fire Transforms") and Anchor 5 (Death and destruction are not hopeless). Scripture interprets itself. Jesus frequently quotes Isaiah[a] and this is significant. The phrase "both soul and body" is used one other time, and it's found in the OT. Jesus likely used it as Isaiah did: "So the Light of Israel will be for a *fire* and his Holy One for a *flame*; It will *burn* and "devour"[b] His *thorns* and his *briers* in *one day*. And it will *consume* the *glory* of his forest and of his fruitful field, *both soul and body*; and they [Assyria] will be *as* when a sick man *wastes away.* ..." (Is 10:17-18) "Both soul and body" is a metaphor implying "entirely" as we just saw in the MSG. The context is similar: a fiery judgment that consumes, i.e., destroys.

Note these distinctions: fire burns the thorns and briers (i.e., sin?) in one day, not endless days; this is not eternity! Assyria's glory (power and riches?) will be destroyed entirely—both soul and body[c] as when a sick person wastes away. Do you think this judgment annihilated Assyria forever? No! Only its selfish, prideful glory was. For Isaiah writes later: "*In that day* Israel will be one of three with Egypt and *Assyria*—a blessing in the midst of the land, whom the Lord of hosts shall bless, saying, "Blessed is Egypt My people, *and Assyria* the work of My hands, and Israel My inheritance." (19:24-5) "So it shall be *in that day*: The great trumpet will be blown; They will come, who are about to perish in the land of *Assyria* ... and *shall worship the Lord* in the holy mount at Jerusalem." (27:13) What great hope Isaiah offers!

Furthermore, God is *not* a terrorist; for truly, had the disciples understood His threat as endless suffering, they would have been consumed by and overwhelmed with terror. Do you think they would have cared in the least, if they were of more value than sparrows or if their hairs were numbered if they had just been threatened with endless torment? Any subsequent words of comfort would have been futile. It's *not* the "fear not" they would remember but His horrendous heart-wrenching threat; it would have overshadowed anything else Jesus would add. And since He *immediately* said, "Do not fear *therefore*," it is impossible that eternal torment was on anyone's mind. Common sense should tell us this. This is further confirmed by His reference to God as our "Father." A loving father always has his children's welfare in mind.

Finally, Jesus said God "can" destroy us, not that He actually would. Though He "can" raise worshippers from stones (Mt 3:9), He does *not* do so; He is merely making a contrast! These several factors preserve my conviction that God's love for all will prevail.

(a) For example: Is 6:9-10; Mt 13:15; Mk 4:12; Lk 8:9-10; Is 29:13; Mt 15:9; Mk 7:7; Is 56:7; Mt 21:13; Mk 11:17; Lk 19:46; Is 13:10; 34:4; Mt 24:29; Mk 13:24; Is 66:24; Mk 9:48; Is 61:1-2; Lk 4:18-19; Is 53:12; Lk 22:37; Is 54:13; Jn 6:45.

(b) Note how Zaphania used the word, "devour" H398: "*All* the earth shall be *devoured* with the fire of my jealousy. For then I will restore ... *that* they *all* may call on ... the Lord, to serve Him." (Zep 3:8-9) God *devours* to restore!

(c) That "both soul and body" is used for a whole nation affirms its metaphorical nature in Matthew 10:28.

[486] See also RSV; ESV; PME; CEB; CJB; etc.

[487] Judgment is always measured—according to deeds. See Anchor 6, "The Written Law."

[488] Note the previous verses: "If anyone desires to come after Me, let him deny himself and take up his cross, and follow Me. For whoever desires to save his life [*psuchē* G5590] will lose it, but whoever loses his life [*psuchē*] for My sake will *find* it." (Mt 16:24-25) The Greek word for "life" here is the same as "soul" (NKJV) in the next verse! To switch the meaning from "life" to "soul" in the second clause of the same passage is misleading. The warning is not about losing an "eternal" soul but about wasting our lives. He's inviting us to join Him in His world mission. To turn from such a noble task for the selfish pleasures of this short life will bring great loss, sorrow and regret at the resurrection. Let us not waste our lives!

[489] Mt 19:21

[490] "If anyone's work is burned, he will suffer loss; but ... will be saved, yet so as through fire." (1Cor 3:15; Cf. 10-15)

[491] Acts 3:1 (NIV); Jn 6:35, 11:25; 1Jn 1:1

[492] The context relates to over-comers (v. 5). Even if we don't overcome or endure, or we deny Him and thus forfeit the privilege of reigning with Christ (2Tm 2:12), or are found faithless; He ultimately remains faithful to Himself—to all His promises. He cannot be otherwise. (2Tm 2:13) See Anchor 8.

[493] Rom 11:17, 23-26

[494] See Anchor 9, Promise 3.

[495] NTAT: "Has no excuse throughout the age [fn: "Or until the Age [to come]"], but is answerable for a transgression in the Age [fn: An "aeonian transgression": perhaps "answerable for an age-long transgression."]."

[496] Mk 3:29 ... REB: "Hath no forgiveness, unto times age-abiding, But is guilty of an age-abiding sin." MYLT reads: "has not forgiveness—to the age, but is in danger of age-during judgment." TNT: "continues not having a release on into the Age. But rather, he continues existing being one caught within an eonian effect of a mistake." CLT: "is having no pardon for the eon, but is liable to the eonian penalty for the sin." The Online Interlinear: "not is-having pardon into the eon, but liable is of eonian

judging."[a] The 2001 Translation: "won't be forgiven through the age."[b] ABP: "has not forgiveness into the eon." Note: I asked Jonathan Mitchell (TNT translator), if "has never forgiveness" in Mk 3:29 is remotely possible since so many translations state that. He replied, "Gerry, I say emphatically, 'NO!' If you will note from the *Blueletterbible* link you sent, to arrive at the idiomatic rendering "never" took the combining of the entire Greek phrase. This is what the common translations do. They presume that by using this and similar phrases that the Greek speakers of the 1st century meant what we mean in English by our word "never." This is interpretation, injecting our concept of "never" into the Greek.

[a] www.Scripture4all.org
[b] www.2001translation.com

[497] Or blindly attributing to Jesus such a spirit (Mt 12:24-25, 32), which is blasphemy against the Holy Spirit.

[498] Phil 2:9-11

[499] Or *Immeasurable, Infinite or Limitless* riches of His grace: AMP, AMPC, CJB, CSB, ESV, HCSB, ISV, JB, NABRE, NRSV, RSV.

[500] Eph 2:7. See Anchor 10, "New Jerusalem."

[501] See Anchor 6, "The Written Law."

[502] This sentence is in the present tense: See NAS, CJB, DLNT, HCSB, CLT, TLV, NTAT, TNT, ABP, K. S.Wuest NT, etc.

[503] The "gate" is primarily a present state of being, i.e., the kingdom of God *within* us (Lk 17:20-21), defined as righteousness [*goodness*—NLT, MSG, TLB], *peace* and *joy*." (Rom 14:17) God calls us to responsible action—in sacrificial love for others—in His Kingdom right now: "Let your light so shine before men, that they may see your good works and glorify your Father in heaven. ... [And pray:] Your kingdom come. Your will be done on earth as it is in heaven." (Mt 5:16; 6:10) Progress in salvation should be "evident to all." (1Tm 4:9-16) Note: true progress relates to our motives—not the motivation from future rewards but seeing others blessed for its own sake. A loving, selfless attitude is inevitable as we grow more and more into the likeness of Christ—His heart for hurting people becomes ours. (Mt 9:36; Jn 11:35; 1Jn 4:18)

[504] NTAT; "will not be strong enough." (CLT)

[505] Lk 13:23-30

[506] Note how Jesus concludes His parable. "*Indeed* there are last who will be first and ... first ... last." This statement offers us great hope. It affirms that these judgments are *not* endless. The context is undeniable. R.T. Lancaster says it was "a rabbinic expression for placing one's disciples on the ban ... ordinarily from 7 to 30 days, but in this case ... the Messianic Era. ... Some whom we would have expected to be of first rank in the kingdom will occupy the lowest station, and some whom we would have expected to be least in the kingdom will occupy the highest station." He adds: "According to Jewish belief about the Messianic Age,

the LORD will host a great banquet in Jerusalem. ... The resurrected righteous will be present at the table. ... The rejected disciples, barred from the Messianic Era, will see the great banquet of Messiah, but they will not find a place at the table. ... They themselves will be thrown out ... to wait out the Messianic Era in *Gehenna*."[a]

[a] R.T. Lancaster. *The Chronicles of the Messiah*. Bk 3. 2nd Ed. The Torah Club. First Fruits of Zion, 2014. 1030-33. www.torahclub.ffoz.org.

[507] TNT reads, "weeping and grinding (or gnashing) of the teeth (= the sorrow and regret) will be [out] there, in that place." The JB reads the last clause: "turned outside." Phillips: "excluded, outside."

[508] Ps 30:4-5. Joy follows mourning!

[509] Lk 13:34-35

[510] It's about a place of honor in Christ's future reign. See 2Tm 2:12; 1Cor 3:10-15. More: www.HopeForAllFellowship.com/Ruling

[511] Jn 4:42; 1Jn 4:14

[512] "And so *all* Israel [the first—Acts 3:25-26] *will be saved*, as it is written: 'The Deliverer will come out of Zion, and He will turn away ungodliness from Jacob ... For as you [the last] were once disobedient to God, yet have now obtained mercy through their disobedience, even so these also [the first] have now been disobedient, that through the mercy shown you they also may obtain mercy. For God has committed them *all* [first and last] to disobedience, that He might have mercy on *all*.'" (Rom 11:26-32)

[513] The Expanded Bible

[514] Ez 22:15-16, 18, 21-22. Israel is "melted," i.e., purified to remove their "filthiness completely," so they would become the people and nation they were called to be: a blessing to the whole world. (Gn 12:3; 18:18; 22:18; 26:4; 28:14; Acts 3:25-26; Gal 3:8)

David also referred to a *furnace* that purifies silver seven times. (Ps 12:6)

Isaiah wrote, "Hear ... Israel ... Who swear by the name of the Lord ... But not in truth or in righteousness ... I have made you hear new things from this time, even hidden things, and you did not know them ... from long ago your ear was not opened. For I knew that you would deal very treacherously, and were called a transgressor from the womb. For My name's sake I will defer My anger, and for My praise I will restrain it from you, so that I do not cut you off. Behold, I have refined you, but not as silver; I have tested you in the *furnace of affliction*. For My own sake ... I will do it ... Listen to Me, O Jacob, and Israel, My called: I am He, I am the First, I am also the Last." (Is 48:1-12)

Elsewhere in Scripture we learn that what God does for Israel will subsequently be granted to all. See Anchor 9, Promise 3. (Rom 11:26) See Anchors 2-4.

[515] Mt 15:24; Acts 3:26

[516] Recall the limited duration of *aionios* in Anchor 4.

[517] See Anchor 6 which establishes the limited nature of God's justice.

[518] *Dikē* is defined as justice (the principle, a decision, or its execution).[a]
[a] Strong, James. Ibid. 24.

[519] Vincent, Marvin. Ibid. Vol. 1. 715.

[520] "And your sister Sodom ... and her daughters shall be restored as they were from the beginning." (Ez 16:55 ABP) See Anchor 5, "Hope in Destruction," number 5.

[521] See Anchor 4, "Greek *Gehenna*," Point 1, Mt 5 :25-26.

[522] Lk 3:5; Is 40:3-5

[523] "For I am persuaded that neither death nor life, nor angels nor principalities nor powers, nor things present nor things to come, nor height nor depth, nor *any other created thing*, [which include all chasms] shall be able to separate us from the love of God which is in Christ Jesus our Lord." (Rom 8:38-39)

[524] "Death and *Hades* delivered up the dead who were in them." (Rv 20:13)

[525] All the earth shall be devoured with fire that they all may call on and serve the Lord." (Zep 3:8-9) "The fierce anger of the Lord will not turn back *until* He has performed and *until* He has accomplished the intent of His heart. In the latter days you will understand this." (Jer 30:24 NAS; repeated in 23:20) See Anchor 2.

[526] "The fire is not *going* out." (CLT) "*continues not being* extinguished." (TNT)

[527] Strong, James. Ibid. 14, G762.

[528] In the following 44 translations, Mark 9:43 does not include the word "never.": ABP, AMP, ASV, CEB, CJB, CLT, Darby, DLNT, DRA, ESV, ESVUK, GW, HCSB, HNV, ISV, JB, TNT, LB, LEB, MSG, Mounce, NABRE, NAS, NEB, NET, NLT, NLV, NOG, NOAB, NRSV, NRSVACE, NRSVCE, OJB, PHILLIPS, REB, RSV, RSVCE, TLB, NTAT, SNT, VOICE, WEB, WEY, MYLT. The KJV is not consistent. It translates *asbestos* as "unquenchable" twice with "never" and twice without it.

[529] "*Everyone* will be seasoned [*purified*—GNT] with *fire*, and every sacrifice will be seasoned with salt. Salt is *good*." (Mk 9:49-50) The unquenchable fire is something good that everyone must experience. And since everyone experiences it, it cannot be endless. See Anchor 2.

[530] Late president and founder of the Pittsburgh Bible Institute.

[531] "Sulphur [brimstone] was sacred to the deity among the ancient Greeks; and was used to fumigate, to purify, to cleanse and consecrate to the deity; for this purpose they burned it in their incense. In Homer's Iliad (16:228), one is spoken of as purifying a goblet with fire and brimstone. The verb derived from *Theion* is *Theioo*, which means to hallow, to make divine or to dedicate to a god (see Liddell and Scott Greek-English Lexicon, 1897 Ed.)."[a]

(a) Pridgeon, Charles H. *Is Hell Eternal or Will God's Plan Fail?* Third Ed. The Evangelization Society of the Pittsburgh Bible Institute, n.p. 1931. Chapter 11.

532 Refers to Christians tortured (*tumpanizō* G5178) for their faith. Heb 11: 35

533 Mt 14:24

534 Mk 6:48

535 2Pt 2:7 (*troubled* NLV, NCV, CEV, ERV, ICB, NTE, TLV). EXB: *troubled* [distressed; or oppressed].

536 Pridgeon adds, "The original idea of *basanizo* is 'to put to the test by rubbing on a touchstone,' to test some metal that looked like gold to find whether it was real or not. The meaning and usage harmonizes with the idea of divine purification and the torment which is the test to find whether there has been any change in the sufferer."(a)

(a) Pridgeon, Ibid.

537 Atomic number 16.

538 Davis, Donald and Randall Detro. *Fire and Brimstone The History of Melting Louisiana's Sulphur.* Baton Rouge, Louisiana Geological Survey. 1992. "Sulfur History." Paragraph four. www.georgiagulfsulfur.com/sulfur/history

I credit George Sarris for informing me of this source.

539 *basanizo* G928

540 Rv 14:10b TNT

541 Rv 14:10. Also, "The Ancient One sat down to judge. ... He sat on a fiery throne, ... and a river of fire was pouring out flowing from His presence. ... " (Dn 7:9-10 NLT) "If I make my bed in hell [*Sheol*], behold, *You are there*." (Ps 139:8)

542 "And the dead were judged *according to their works.* ... and Death and *Hades delivered up the dead* who were in them. And they were judged, each one *according to his works.*" (Rv 20:12-13) "*According to their works* [repeated twice here] and *Hades* delivering up the dead," clearly show the limited nature of this judgment. It is not endless! See Anchor 6, "The Written Law" and "The Written Law Revealed in the Metaphorical Lake of Fire." As well, Anchor 2—Hope in Fire.

543 Though "lake of fire" is not stated here, most assume it's referred to. For more on "*to ages of ages:*" see Anchor 4, "Greek *Eis Tous Aiōnas Tōn Aiōnōn.*"

544 Rv 18:17-19; 19:2-3. This judgment, quoted as lasting *forever and ever* in most translations, only lasted *one* hour—and is called God's *righteous* judgment (19:2), harmonizing with Anchors 2, 3 and 6.

545 Repeated 3 times—vs. 18:10, 17, 19.

546 For more see Anchor 4, "*Eis tous aiōnas ton aiōnon.*"

547 "And they shall go forth and look upon the corpses of the men who have transgressed against me, for their worm does not die and their fire is not quenched. They shall be an abhorrence to all flesh." (Is 66:24)

[548] This is noteworthy because the objective of their book was to defend the idea of eternal torment. And furthermore, Dr. Sprinkle, the key researcher for *Erasing Hell*, has since changed his view about endless torment.[a]

[a] Phillip. "Co-Author of 'Erasing Hell'—Changing His Position on Hell?" *Christian Universalism*. 22 Mar 2013. www.christianuniversalism.com.

[549] Chan, Francis and Preston Sprinkle. *Erasing Hell*. Colorado Springs: David C Cook, 2011. 89.

[550] See Anchor 6, "The Written Law."

[551] " ... into *hell fire* where 'their *worm* does not die and the *fire is not quenched*.' For *everyone* will be seasoned [purified—GNT] with fire." (Mk 9:47-49) Since these three things affect everyone, they cannot be elements of endless punishment; but instead, agents of transformation!

"Worm" is defined as "worm, maggot or grub which sometimes feeds on dead bodies."[a] Fire and maggots were part of the repugnant conditions in the Jerusalem garbage dump of *Gehenna*, where bodies of criminals were dumped to their utmost disgrace. Dr. A. Nyland writes, "*Gehenna* was ... the Jerusalem rubbish dump. ... Smoke went up from it at all times as the rubbish was burning continually. It was full of maggots, and the bodies of the worst criminals were thrown there. Josiah used it for the burning of offal. It used to be the site of child sacrifice to Molech."[b]

Fire and maggots are purifying agents which destroy disease carrying organisms. All this suggests that the undying worm metaphorically depicts the purifying nature of *Gehenna* fire. Maggots are relentless until all dross and decayed matter are consumed. Similarly, God is relentless in removing all impurity from His children!

[a] Zodhiates, Spiros. Ibid. G4663. 1299

[b] The Source New Testament. Matthew 5:22 footnote.

[552] Zodhiates defines *gár* as "a causative particle standing always after one or more words in a clause and expressing the reason for what has been before, affirmed or implied."[a]

[a] Zodhiates, Spiros. Ibid. G1063. 357

[553] Mt 5:16

[554] A selfish life naturally leads to great loss of privilege and reward, not endless punishment: "*If* we endure, we shall *also reign* with Him. *If* we deny Him, He also will deny us [the privilege of reigning with Him]. If we are faithless, He remains faithful [to His promises to forgive, discipline and purify us. Why?]; He cannot deny Himself [as the Good Shepherd and Savior of the World]." (2Tm 2:12-13)

Paul also wrote: "Some of the branches were broken off ... because of unbelief. ... And ... if they do not continue in unbelief will be grafted in, for *God is able to graft them in again*. ... And so *all Israel will be saved*, as it is written: ' ... He will turn away ungodliness from Jacob ... when I take away their sins.'" (Rom 11:17, 20, 23, 26-27)

Branches that were broken off, are grafted in again unto salvation! Note what salvation means: "*removing ungodliness.*" (NAS)

Paul further says: "Let each one take heed how he builds. ... Now if anyone builds ... with gold ... wood ... straw, each one's work ... will be revealed by fire; and the fire [burning] will test each one's work, of what sort it is. If anyone's work ... endures, he will receive a reward. If anyone's work is burned, he will suffer loss; but he himself will be saved, yet so as through fire." (1Cor 3:10-15) God's judgment fire, whatever the source, is not endless punishment but a purifying and testing process. See Anchor 2.

We must compare Scripture with Scripture, taking into account their various metaphorical nuances, in order to understand many passages. Individual verses are not islands to themselves but part of a larger story. "Be diligent to present yourself approved to God, a worker who does not need to be ashamed, rightly dividing the word of truth." (2Tm 2:15)

[555] Heb 6:4-6

[556] "But if it yields thorns and thistles it is worthless [in one sense only—not ultimately—GB], in fact very *nearly* a curse, whose end is to be burned." (Heb 6:8 NTAT) See the transforming nature of God's metaphorical fires in Anchor 2.

[557] See note 275.

[558] Mt 3:9; Lk 3:8

[559] Heb 6:4-6 "For it is impossible—regarding those who ... having fallen away—to *restore* them to a changed [repentant—GB] heart." (NTAT) "It is impossible to *restore* the changed [unrepentant—GB] heart of the one who has fallen from faith." (VOICE). But God's ultimate purpose is *not to restore* unrepentant hearts, but to give us *new* hearts which need no repentance! See Anchor 8, "God Can Change Anyone."

[560] Our loving Father's justice, in His judgments to come, will allow His rebellious children to go through whatever is necessary to bring them to repentance—Lk 15:11-32. His love never fails. (1Cor 13:8)

[561] See Anchors 6, 7, 8, 9 and 10.

[562] He would not have entrusted such a critical assignment to a few people with hellish visions. Jesus said, "Why do you not even on your own initiative judge what is right?" Lk 12:57 (NAS). Paul said test all things and hold fast to what is good. (1Thes 5:21)

[563] Jn 16:13. See also Lk 24:27, 31, 32, 45.

[564] What greater terror can be inflicted on a human being? See Lk 2:10; Rom 10:15; Acts 10:36; Phil 4:4; 1Pt 1:8 NAS.

[565] Jn 14:27

[566] 2Cor 10:5

[567] How? They impede us from obeying Jesus in these exhortations.

[568] The ABP reads: "It was good to him if that man was not born." MYLT: "good it were for him if that man had not been born." TNT: "It was continuing being beautiful for Him [i.e., for the Son of the Man]—if THAT MAN was not brought to birth!"

[569] The Christian community, as a whole, believes aborted and stillborn babies experience resurrection life. That is far better than to never have been conceived. But of far greater importance is this stark fact: Better that no human should ever be born if an endless punishment weighed in the balance.

[570] www.HopeForAllFellowship.com/Judas

[571] Lk 14:26; Mk 8:33. Of course Jesus wants us to love our families, but our deepest love should be for our Father.

[572] See Anchor 2.

[573] Gn 25:34; 27:34, 38

[574] God abundantly blessed Esau after he lost his birthright. He commanded 400 men (Gn 32:6) and claimed to have "plenty." (Gn 33:9 NIV) And when Jacob first saw Esau's face, after having deceived their father in getting Esau's blessing and birthright, Jacob said he saw the "face of God." In addition to Esau's acquiring wealth, he exemplified Christ's Spirit in extending mercy and grace (spiritual riches) to Jacob (the deceiver), who really deserved his wrath. (Gn 33:10)

[575] See Anchor 6.

[576] Gn 18:25; Lk 12:57; Thes 5:21

[577] Jesus said that though we are "evil," we know how to give *good* gifts. (Mt 7:11) We all know good from evil—just from unjust punishment. Thus we are responsible before God to: a) listen to His voice in our conscience when reading *human translations* and *interpretations* of the ancient Scriptures; b) wait until He opens our understanding and fills our heart with peace; c) remember: "the letter kills, but the Spirit gives life. (2Cor 3:6). Jesus said to His disciples, regarding a very severe judgment: "But I say to you that it shall be more tolerable for the land of Sodom in the day of judgment than for you. At *that* time Jesus answered and said, 'I thank You, Father ... that You have hidden these things [about judgment] from the wise and prudent and have revealed them to babes. Even so, Father, for so it seemed good in Your sight.'" (Mt 11:24-26; cp Rom 11:32-33) Only God reveals the truth about His judgments.

[578] "Wicked" is unjustified. See Anchor 6, "The Unwritten Law," Point 4.

[579] "The heart is *deep* beyond all things, and man is, who shall know him? I the Lord am examining hearts ... to give to each according to his ways, and according to the fruits of their practices." (Jer 17:9 ABP) See Anchor 6, "The Unwritten Law," Point 4.

[580] Rom 1:32. That is not to say that there are no gray areas. But overall, the vast majority of sound-minded people agree on basic morals.

[581] For example: purgatory, slavery, capital punishment, politics, role of women, Sabbath laws, baptism rituals, the Holy Eucharist, communion ordinances, divorce,

remarriage, tithing, relevance of miracles, spiritual gifts, music in church, speaking in tongues, prophecy, "free will," sovereignty, eternal security, sexual issues, age of accountability, purpose of parables, literal or spiritual Israel, the last days, the rapture, purpose of Satan, demonic possession, bearing arms, patriotism, taxation, etc.

[582] See Anchor 1, "The Early Church."

[583] The ancient fathers, while embracing the real good news, perceived the danger of "premature" truth and often exercised the "doctrine of reserve," the policy of not revealing what they truly believed about limited judgment for fear society might plunge into lawlessness and vice. "Truth" out of season, they reasoned, would do more harm than good. Rev. Thomas Allin wrote, "It [was] the fashion to confine the doctrine of reserve to the duty of suppressing a truth deemed inexpedient to disclose."[a] He goes on to give many examples from the fathers' own words. This explains why some Fathers acknowledge it in some sources and not others—leading modern scholars to differ with Jukes, Allin, Beecher and others on this point—not taking it into consideration.
[a] Allin, Thomas. Ibid. 85.

[584] Jn 16:12

[585] Grace is the greatest theme in the Church today—just observe the words we sing in our worship services and Christian radio, also the sermons we preach and the books we write. It seems the Holy Spirit is doing something amazing in our midst, revealing God's great love and mercy. It's not surprising then, that the time has come for the Church to examine with great diligence, the Biblical and historical evidence for the doctrine of endless punishment, as it bears directly on our understanding of grace and God's character! Otherwise, our message is contradictory. A century ago, Dr. Edward Beecher wrote, "Although the inertia of that vast body called the Church is almost unconquerable, when God's time comes, when the Church is holier and in more intimate communion with him, their apathy [about endless punishment] will pass away, and they will penetrate the whole subject to its very depths."[a] This is already happening in our time!
[a] Beecher, Edward. Ibid. Ch 36.

[586] "Blessed are you poor, for yours is the kingdom of God. Blessed are you who hunger now, for you shall be filled. Blessed are you who weep now, for you shall laugh Lk 6:20-21." Certainly it would not be a blessing, if endless suffering in hell awaited most of the world's suffering people. The teaching of an endless hell strips this passage of any true comfort it might bring to a hurting world—thus revealing its fallacy.

[587] Rom 8:18 (TLB)

[588] 1Jn 4:8, 16

[589] Eccl 3:11

[590] Rv 21:4

[591] Jer 23:20 ["and intents"—30:24]

[592] Jer 30:24

[593] Is 2:2 (NIV)

[594] Many think we are living in those "last days." That could be, since we are seeing long held and horrific misconceptions about God, rooted in the dark ages, eroding away. More and more, believers in Christ are embracing a God of infinite grace, mercy and love. This is an exciting time in church history.

[595] Jesus did not come to found an "ism" but to save the world. The word "universal" is actually a Biblical concept—it expresses the scope of God's love for all humanity and the effectiveness of Jesus' sacrifice. Jesus is Lord of lords, King of kings— Savior of the world. (Jn 4:42) He is *the* Way, *the* Truth and *the* Life; *no one* comes to the Father except through Him. Most who share our high view of Jesus don't see themselves as Universalists; some however, regard their faith as "Christian," "Biblical," or "Evangelical" universalism—see www.christianuniversalism.com My friends Gary and Michelle Amirault hosts an encyclopedic website which has greatly blessed me over the years: www.tentmaker.org. They refer to their faith as the Victorious Gospel! Gary explains Christian Universalism very well: www.tentmaker.org/universalism.htm

[596] Hart is a recognized modern Bible scholar *and* not biased by a belief in endless punishment. See pages 537-548 to learn why two Greek terms used to support endless punishment actually affirm the contrary. See note 128 for Hart's bio. His introduction explains his translation. Brad Jersak, an author and theologian I appreciate, offers a helpful review of this translation: www.HopeForAllFellowship.com/NTReview/

[597] References I use: TNT,[a] CLT,[b] MYLT, SNT, NAS, ABP, DSB, Eight Translation N.T., Online Bibles: Biblegateway.com, Blueletterbible.org, Biblehub.com/interlinear. Note: we do not need to be scholars to compare translations. "Be *diligent ... rightly dividing* the word of truth." (2Tm 2:15)

[a] *The New Testament: God's Message ...* Paperback by Jonathan Paul Mitchell. This New Testament includes the various possibilities hidden in the Greek text not evident to English-only readers. It lays out all the options without limiting the number of words needed to get the meaning across. Amazon.

[b] The *Concordant Literal Translation* consistently links one English word to each Greek word, enabling the seeker of truth to more accurately compare one passage with another. In this way one can develop a natural sense for a word's meaning. Amazon.

[598] Lk 24:32

[599] Jesus says, "Come to Me, all you who labor and are heavy laden, and I will give you rest. Take My yoke [instructions and guidance] upon you and learn from Me [from His example], for I am gentle and lowly in heart, and you will find rest for your souls. For My yoke is easy and My burden is light." (Mt 11:28-29) Jesus is our Creator ... Entered our world 2,000 years ago as a human being so we could know Him ... Died on a cruel cross for the world's sin—Revealing God's unimaginable love for every human being. Having never sinned, He suffered for us all. What a Savior—the world's Savior! Jesus is a good and gentle Shepherd ... Who invites us—we who are weighed down by guilt

and the difficulties of life—to come and find rest and peace in His presence. And because He truly cares for us—living in Him is not a burden. We just need to cast our cares on Him every day. His key command (or yoke) is that we love others as ourselves which He empowers us to do. This brings great meaning and purpose to our lives.

Jesus is an intimate friend who is always with us. He desires to talk with us if we'll listen. It helps me to talk out loud with Him, especially when I'm walking outdoors surrounded by His beautiful creation. Listen to His still small voice speaking to your heart. He will let you know when you have mistreated someone or were unkind. And when you mess up, tell Him—He'll assure you He still loves you. He wants you to know when you have hurt someone so you'll be more careful next time. Admit it—confess it, then brush the dust off and move on. Life is about one thing: loving God through loving others. That only happens as we yield to His Spirit working in us.

Read the New Testament a little at a time. Don't make it a burden but a special joy in your life. There you'll see the life of Jesus and His followers: how they lived and what they said. Most of it is easy to follow. As the beauty of Jesus and His words (along with those of His followers) shine forth—they will fill your heart with light, peace, comfort and purpose. And like those who heard His first public sermon, you too will marvel at His gracious words.

Jesus said where two or three come together in His name, He is in our midst in a special way through each other. Note He said two or three, not 20 or 30 or 200. We all need a friend—someone we can trust and confide in—who will encourage us in our faith and lovingly accept us as we are. Why do you think Jesus sent out His 72 disciples in two's? The Apostle Paul always journeyed with a companion. One way to make such a friend (or friends) is to reach out to others. Share this book with the people in your life: family, friends, co-workers, classmates ... You may find someone who, like you, is thrilled about God's unlimited unfailing love for every person. You won't know unless you share it. See my video: www.hopeforallfellowship.com/Connect

Please be careful to love and accept everyone no matter what they believe. Some people will strongly disagree with your view of God. Love them anyway. Five times in Jesus' heart-wrenching prayer—on the eve of His crucifixion, He asked His Father to make us one. It meant everything to Him, and so it should be a priority for us, too. If you would like to learn more about our life in Jesus, call or email us. (800) 254-1334.

[600] 1Pt 1:8

[601] One who searches the Scriptures carefully for themselves to determine if what has been taught them is, in fact, Scripturally accurate. (Acts 17:11)

CPSIA information can be obtained
at www.ICGtesting.com
Printed in the USA
LVHW04s0243150918
590208LV00004B/26/P